BEYOND BILAL

Black Muslims in The East

MUSTAFA BRIGGS

Edited by Ali Hussain & Omar Laaroussi.

First Printing, 2023

ISBN

Mustafa Briggs & Co. Publishing www.mustafabriggs.com

To Yasmina,

With deepest gratitude, I thank you,

For your belief in me,

For your unwavering support,

For your patience with me on my journey

For recognizing the potential within my soul and

For challenging me to actualise it

CONTENTS

INTRODUCTION

In the introduction of 'Beyond Bilal: Black History in Islam', I detailed the evolution of the project from a lecture series which I presented in multiple universities into a book. In October 2018, coinciding with UK Black History Month, I embarked on an unparalleled university tour, visiting twenty institutions. This whirlwind journey had me travelling extensively by train to present "Beyond Bilal" to students all across the UK. It's noteworthy that all these invitations came from these universities due to requests from the students and student societies themselves.

This UK tour during October 2018 was succeeded by a USA tour in February 2019. There, I had the privilege to present 'Beyond Bilal' at esteemed institutions including the Islamic Center of New York University, Harvard, Yale, Brown, the University of Pennsylvania, and several others.

The momentum continued as 'Beyond Bilal' was soon complemented by 'Before Malcolm X: The History of Islam in The Americas' and 'Daughters of Fatima: African Female Scholarship in the Islamic Tradition'. Both these projects were toured in October 2019 throughout the UK, and later in the USA & Canada in February 2020, aligning with their respective Black History Months.

Upon my return to Cairo in March 2020, the world grappled with an unparalleled challenge. The sudden emergence of COVID-19 and the resulting lockdowns significantly altered modern history's trajectory, prompting a collective pause and time for introspection. Airports and borders shut down, stringent lockdowns were implemented, and we found ourselves confined to our homes for months. The bustling communities we had once been a part of were compelled to reshape their existence in a predominantly digital realm. Platforms like Clubhouse thrived, fostering extensive cross-continental conversations and debates.

During this time, my friend Mohammed Isaaq introduced me to a potential avenue I hadn't previously considered. He reached out to me to connect him with my graphic designer, Islaam Yasin, for his upcoming course, 'Knowing Yourself.' This Islāmic Psychology Programme draws inspiration from the ancient Hellenic medicine's four temperaments, as understood by traditional Islāmic scholarship. It was during a phone call that Isaaq then told me, "I'm utilising CrowdCast for my course, where people can register, and you can live-stream classes. These sessions are archived for future viewing. Given your travel restrictions, why not transition 'Beyond Bilal' online?" Encouraged by his idea and with his assistance in setting up my account, I began teaching my previous lectures online. Additionally, I introduced two fresh lectures: 'Africans in Asia' and 'Black History in the Arab World'.

During my presentation of 'Beyond Bilal', I observed a fascinating trend, that most attendees keen on learning about Black History in Islām weren't just Black Muslims, but many were of Arab and Asian heritage. It appeared that after years of perceiving Islām through a singular lens, those of Arab and Asian heritage were eager to explore fresh perspectives and information previously unfamiliar to them. I further realised I had responsibility, as a significant portion of mosques and Muslim student organisations in North America and the UK (where I was frequently invited) comprised these demographics. If I was conveying previously unknown and fascinating information, I wanted to convey that Black Muslim history didn't just shape Africa and the West, but also profoundly influenced the history, dissemination, and evolution of Islām in Asia and the Arab world.

While many anticipate learning about the influence of Black Muslims on the history and trajectory of Islām in Africa and, subsequently, the African diaspora in North and South America, fewer are aware of the rich tapestry of Black contributions to ancient Arabian civilisation. Some of Ancient Arabia's most celebrated poets, warriors, explorers, and conquerors were Black. Furthermore, Black intellectuals and revolutionaries significantly shaped the

Islāmic Empires of the Middle Ages. Prominent figures, including the inaugural Muftīs of Makkah and Egypt, along with pivotal narrators of ḥadīth and early luminaries in the Islāmic tradition, were of Black heritage.

Moreover, whilst my previous book offered a comprehensive exploration of Islām's spread in West Africa, this new volume aims to shine a light on East Africa. It uncovers tales of formidable kingdoms in India, Pakistan, and Bangladesh, which were directed and sculpted by East African monarchs, saints, and explorers. This book before you endeavours to chronicle the establishment of those vibrant communities and the enduring impact their legacies continue to imprint upon those regions to this day.

In conclusion, the narrative of Black Muslims transcends geographical boundaries and epochs. It weaves a vast and intricate tale that stretches from the heartlands of Africa to the arid landscapes of Arabia and the vibrant heartlands of Asia. I hope this book stands as a testament to the enduring and significant contributions of Black Muslims to the annals of Islāmic history, underscoring the profound depth, diversity, and interconnectedness of the Muslim world. Whilst replicating the success and impact of 'Beyond Bilal' may be a tall order, my aspiration for this second volume is that it proves to be equally enlightening and captivating. I hope it resonates with you as deeply as its predecessor, furthering our collective journey towards realising the profound wisdom of the Qur'ānic verse, "*Oh*

Mankind! Indeed, We created you from a male and a female, and made you into peoples and tribes so that you may know one another." [Qur'ān 49:13].

Chapter 1:
THE CROWS OF THE ARABS

It is a guiding principle in Islāmic theology that the miracle of every prophet or messenger of God aligns with the preeminent social phenomenon of the society he is sent to. Moses (Mūsā) preached in the occult-ridden world of Pharaonic Egypt, a world enamoured by witchcraft, magic, and various esoteric sciences, and, thus, was given the miraculous ability to perform displays of power that far exceeded the Egyptian occultists, such as transforming his staff into a snake, altering the waters of the Nile into blood, and spliting the Sea of Reeds. Jesus (ʿĪsā) was given the power to heal the sick and raise the dead amidst the communities of Roman Judea which were heavily influenced to place significant importance on physicians and medical sciences by the Ancient Greek and Latin worlds.

Thus, when discussing the miracle of the Prophet Muḥammad ﷺ, unanimously accepted as the Qur'ān itself, we must understand that the context of the Prophet's miracle— known as 'The Recitation' (the closest translation to the original Arabic word 'Qur'ān')—is rooted in pre-Islāmic Arabian society's emphasis on the mastery of the Arabic language that was expressed through poetry and prose. Steeped in the spoken word, the greatest heroes of that culture were not only denoted by skill in the sword and spear, but also by their eloquence of language. Therefore, such fame was given to the renowned poet-warriors of Jāhiliyyah that their masterful poetic odes hung on the doors of the Ka'bah before the advent of Islām.

Among these celebrated warrior poets sat the brazenly named 'Aghribat al-'Arab' or 'the Crows of the Arabs', named such due to their extremely dark complexions and their sub-Saharan African lineages. Many of them were either the sons of East African women and Arab men or solely of African heritage. It is therefore fitting to begin this book—which aims to explore the Black Muslim History of Asia and the Arab World—with these distinguished Black figures who left such an indelible mark on Arab culture and history.

Ibn Manẓūr, a renowned lexicographical scholar of the Arabic language, notes in his book 'Lisān al-'Arab' that the Arab Crows include 'Antarah, Khufāf ibn Nudbah and 'Abdullāh ibn Khāzim, Abū 'Umayr ibn Al-Ḥubāb, Sulayk ibn Sulakah, Hishām ibn 'Uqbah ibn Abī Mu'īṭ, 'Umayr ibn Abī 'Umayr ibn Al-Ḥubāb from the tribe of Sulaym,

Hammām ibn Muṭarraf from the tribe of Taghlib, and Muntashir ibn Wahb al-Bāhilī, Maṭar ibn Awfā al-Māzinī, Tȧabbaṭa Sharra, and Al-Shanfarā. The impact of these black poets of pre-Islāmic Arabia and their successors throughout Arab civilisation's history was such that the renowned Egyptian poet and professor, Dr. Abduh Badawi, published 'Al-Shuʿarāʾ as-Sūd wa Khasāʾiṣuhum fī ish-Shiʿri il-ʿArabī' (The Black Poets and Their Characteristics in Arabic Poetry) in 1973, compiling the biographies and poetic works of 24 of these poets.

In this chapter, we will examine some of these influential historical figures their roles and contributions, as mentioned by Ibn Manẓūr and in Professor Abduh's study, to Arab poetry before delving into the origins and impact of Black presence on the Arabian Peninsula.

The first poet we will examine is the semi legendary figure whose name and story evoke the same familiarity and emotions in the Arab world as Shakespeare's 'Romeo and Juliet' does so in the West, ʿAntarah.

ʿAntarah ibn Shaddād al-ʾAbsī

Ibn ʿAbd Rabbih, a renowned 9th-century Arab writer and poet from Cordoba in Spain, stated in his seminal work, 'Al-ʿIqd al-Farīd' (The Precious Necklace), which aimed to encompass "all that a well-informed person had to know in order to pass in (Arab) society as a cultured and refined individual",

"The Arabs held such an interest in poetry and valued it so highly that they chose seven lengthy pieces from ancient poetry, wrote them in gold on pieces of Coptic linen, folded them up, and hung them on the curtains covering the Ka'bah. Hence, we speak of 'the golden poem of Imru' al-Qays', 'the golden poem of Zuhayr', etc. The number of the golden poems is seven; they are also called 'The Suspended' (Al-Mu'allaqāt)."

The warrior-poet, 'Antarah ibn Shaddād, later known as 'Antar, was one of the most famous and celebrated authors of one of these seven odes. He was born to Zuhayr, the chief of the Banū 'Abs ethnic group, and Zabībah, an enslaved Ethiopian woman. In pre-Islāmic Arabia, the children of slaves by their masters were also considered slaves (unlike in Islāmic law, where such children were considered free and emancipated their mothers by their birth). Unacknowledged by his father, 'Antar grew up as a slave among the Banū 'Abs until another tribe invaded the Banū 'Abs' lands, triggering intertribal warfare. 'Antar's valiant defence of his tribe and exceptional bravery during the tribal war earned him the recognition of both his father and tribe.

This recognition, however, was not wholehearted. When 'Antar fell in love with his paternal cousin, 'Ablah, and sought her hand in marriage, her father hesitated due to ʿAntar's former slave status. Nonetheless, given ʿAntar's newfound prominence within the tribe and his father's acceptance, ʿAblah's father was unable to outright reject ʿAntar. Instead, he demanded near-impossible tasks from ʿAntar to complete as dowry for his daughter.

ʿAntar not only had to confront these daunting challenges to be accepted as ʿAblah's groom but also faced the scorn and rejection of other men in his tribe who were envious that a former slave held the esteemed position of Banū ʿAbs' most prized knight. This pain from these various levels of opposition motivated ʿAntar to continue fighting and proving himself as the Banū ʿAbs' most fearsome warrior. He was also inspired to express his emotions and reactions to these challenges through some of the most beautiful poetry ever composed in the Arabic language, earning him his legendary renown as one of the Arab world's most famous and celebrated poets.

ʿAntar dealt with various themes in his poetry, such as his passionate love and longing for ʿAblah, the importance of heroism, chivalrous values, overcoming his enemies, the details of his travels in the desert, and his various battles/expeditions. His poetry served as a guidebook, of sorts, on all the attributes that the ideal brave Arab man and warrior should own. It also, of course, touched upon his blackness and the struggles that arrived with it in pre-Islāmic Arab society, as seen in this short excerpt:

أَلَا يَا عَبْلَةُ قَدْ زَادَ التَّصَابِيْ

وَلَجَّ اليَوْمَ قَوْمُكِ فِيْ عَذَابِيْ

Oh 'Ablah, my pain has surely increased,
And today, your people have intensified my torment.

وَظَلَّ هَوَاكِ يَنْمُوْ كُلَّ يَوْمٍ

كَمَا يَنْمُوْ مَشِيْبِيْ فِيْ شَبَابِيْ

Your love continues to grow every day,
Just as my grey hair grows in my youth.

عَتَبْتُ صُرُوْفَ دَهْرِيْ فِيْكِ

حَتّٰى فَنّٰى وَأَبِيْكِ عُمْرِيْ فِي الْعِتَابِ

I have complained about the hardships of my fate with you,
Until your father exhausted my life with reproaches.

وَلَاقَيْتُ الْعِدَا وَحَفِظْتُ قَوْمًا

أَضَاعُوْنِيْ وَلَمْ يَرْعَوْا جَنَابِيْ

I have met enemies and protected people
Who have wasted me and paid no attention to my dignity.

سَلِيْ يَا عَبْلَةُ عَنَّا يَوْمَ زُرْنَا
قَبَائِلَ عَامِرٍ وَبَنِيْ كِلَابِ

Ask, Oh ʿAblah, about the day we visited
The tribes of ʿĀmir and Banū Kilāb.

وَكَمْ مِنْ فَارِسٍ خَلَّيْتُ مُلْقَى
خَضِيْبَ الرَّاحَتَيْنِ بِلَا خِضَابِ

How many knights I left lifeless,
Their bows without strings, and their lances gleaming.

يُحَرِّكُ رِجْلَهُ رُعْبًا وَفِيْهِ
سِنَانُ الرِّمَاحِ يَلْمَعُ كَالشِّهَابِ

Their legs trembled with fear,
And their spearheads shone brilliantly like shooting stars.

قَتَلْنَا مِنْهُمْ مِائَتَيْنِ حُرًّا
وَأَلْفًا فِي الشِّعَابِ وَفِي الهِضَابِ

We killed two hundred free men among them,
And a thousand in the valleys and hills.

The life, story, and poetry of ʿAntar's left such a mark on Arab culture and civilisation that his biography was turned into an epic by Al-Aṣmaʿī, a grammarian and court poet of the famous Caliph, Harūn ar-Rashīd, founder of the House of Wisdom. Al-Aṣmaʿī was described by biographers as being 'a complete master of the Arabic language' and 'the most eminent of all transmitters of the oral history and rare expressions of the language'. Thus, his etching of ʿAntar's story – the black knight of Banū ʿAbs and his beloved ʿAblah – into the annals of Arabian history became a mainstay of Arabic literature, laying the eloquence of one author in service to the other in perpetuity.

Khufāf ibn Nudbah

Khufāf ibn ʿUmayr ibn Al-Ḥārith al-Sulaymī, also known as Khufāf ibn Nudbah, was a pre-Islāmic Arab poet from the famous tribe of Banū Sulaym. It is believed he was born to an Ethiopian woman named Nudbah, although some historians, such as Ibn Ḥajar and Ibn Saʿd, argue that his mother, in fact, was Arab. Despite the debate over his maternal lineage, it is unanimously agreed that he was black and was one of 'the Crows of the Arabs'.

Khufāf ibn Nudbah was one of the most famous poets of pre-Islāmic Arabia, known for his eloquent poetry primarily dealing with themes of chivalry, bravery, and honour. His skilful use of language and vivid imagery captivated audiences and solidified his reputation as a renowned poet of his time.

In addition to his pre-Islāmic fame, Khufāf ibn Nudbah had the opportunity to meet the Prophet Muḥammad ﷺ, embracing Islām before the Conquest of Makkah. He played an active role in the early Islāmic community, carrying the flag of Banū Sulaym during the Conquest of Makkah and taking part in the battles of Ḥunayn and Ṭā'if. He lived until the time of ʿUmar ibn Al-Khaṭṭāb, the second caliph of Islām.

Amongst the distinguishing features of Khufāf ibn Nudbah's poetry was his asceticism. His renunciation of worldly pleasures alongside his steadfastness in his newfound faith prominently featured in a famous poem he wrote denouncing the pagan religion of his tribe and proclaiming his commitment to Islām. Khufāf ibn Nudbah also composed an elegy for Abū Bakr, the first caliph and successor of the Prophet Muḥammad ﷺ after his death. This elegy served as a testament to his deep respect and admiration for the early Islāmic leaders and his ability to capture the emotions and sentiments of his age.

Sulayk ibn Sulakah

Sulayk ibn Sulakah was a pre-Islāmic Arab poet renowned for his daring and adventurous spirit. Born to an Arab father and an Ethiopian mother, Sulayk belonged to the tribe of Banū Kaʿb. He was one of the most famous ṣaʿālik (vagabond poets), who were social outcasts forced to leave their tribes and resort to lives of brigandry and crime. As wayward men orphaned from their ancestral tribes, they often banded together to raid, stealing camels and attacking caravans. These goods were then sold to tribes willing to buy their ill-gotten gains. Some of the ṣaʿālik poets garnered a Robin Hood-esque reputation, celebrated as romantic heroes who stole from the rich and gave to the poor. Their fierce independence and romantic lifestyle shaped them into some of the most renowned and talented poets in the Arab world.

Sulayk's poetry often expressed sorrow over his unfortunate and difficult circumstances, often lamenting his poverty and hunger. His work evokes deep frustration with his poor luck and deep depression. It was also flush with themes of travel, love, and bravery, reflecting the volatile experiences of a vagabond poet.

Al-Shanfarā

Al-Shanfarā, another renowned ṣaʿālik poet, is perhaps best known for his celebrated work, 'Lāmiyyat al-ʿArab'. This preeminent poem stands out in the canon of ṣaʿālik poetry and has been widely read and studied beginning in the pre-Islāmic period. Al-Shanfarā, a name meaning 'he who has large lips', was born to an Arab father from the Azd tribe and an Ethiopian mother.

Despite the existence of various accounts of his biography, a common framework appears across the disparate accounts: Al-Shanfarā's father was killed and he was kidnapped from his tribe and raised by another. Disenchanted with both his birth-tribe and the one that raised him, he vowed to avenge his father's death and his own mistreatment by killing 100 members of the latter tribe. Thus, he embraced the life of a ṣaʿālik, engaging in brigandry and penning many poems about his experiences and philosophy.

Lāmiyyat al-ʿArab is studied worldwide by students of the Arabic language, akin to how Shakespeare is studied by English students. ʿUmar ibn Al-Khaṭṭāb even recommended that the poem be taught to children due to the lofty characteristics it describes. Imām Cheikh Tidiane Cisse, the current Imām of Medina Baye in Senegal, personally shared that Lāmiyyat al-ʿArab was the last work he studied with his grandfather, Shaykh al-Islām Ibrāhīm Niāsse, before his passing. Here are a few excerpts from the Lāmiyah:

أَقِيْمُوْا بَنِيْ أُمِّيْ صُدُوْرَ مَطِيِّكُمْ

فَإِنِّيْ إِلٰى قَوْمٍ سِوَاكُمْ لَأَمْيَلُ

Sons of my mother, rouse your camels now,
For I seek a company other than you.

فَقَدْ حُمَّتِ الْحَاجَاتُ وَاللَّيْلُ مُقْمِرٌ

وَشُدَّتْ لِطِيّاتٍ مَطَايَا وَأَرْحُلُ

Go! You have all you need: the moon shines bright,
The mounts are ready, saddles tightly bound.

وَفِي الْأَرْضِ مَنْأَى لِلْكَرِيْمِ عَنِ الْأَذٰى

وَفِيْهَا لِمَنْ خَافَ الْقِلٰى مُتَعَزَّلُ

This world supplies a refuge for the noble,
A sanctuary for those who fear disdain.

لَعَمْرُكَ مَا فِي الْأَرْضِ ضِيْقٌ عَلٰى امْرِئٍ

سَرٰى رَاغِبًا أَوْ رَاهِبًا وَهُوَ يَعْقِلُ

By your life, there's space on earth for one,
Who wanders, whether looking for or fleeing, with skill.

وَلِيْ دُوْنَكُمْ أَهْلُوْنَ سَيْدٌ عَمَلَّسٌ

وَأَرْقَطُ زُهْلُوْلٌ وَعَرْفَاءُ جَيأَلُ

I have kin closer than you: the swift wolf,
The sleek-coated leopard and the long-haired jackal.

هُمُ الرَّهْطُ لَا مُستَودَعُ السِرِّ ذائِعٌ
لَدَيْهِمْ وَلَا الْجَانِيْ بِمَا جَرَّ يُخْذَلُ

With them, secrets entrusted remain concealed,
Thieves are not ashamed, regardless of their deeds.

وَكُلٌّ أَبِيٌّ باسِلٌ غَيْرَ أَنَّنيْ
إِذَا عَرَضَتْ أُولٰى الطَّرَائِدِ أَبْسَلُ

They are all proud and valiant, yet when we,
Spot the day's first prey, my courage surpasses theirs.

وَإِن مُدَّتِ الْأَيْدِيْ إِلٰى الزَّادِ لَمْ أَكُنْ
بِأَعْجَلِهِم إِذْ أَجَشَعُ الْقَومِ أَعجَلُ

When hands reach for food, I'm not the first,
For the greediest among them are the quickest.

وَمَا ذَاكَ إِلَّا بَسْطَةٌ عَنْ تَفَضُّلٍ
عَلَيْهِمْ وَكَانَ الْأَفضَلَ المُتَفَضِّلُ

That is simply a sign of my grace towards them,
The most noble is he, who shows humility.

وَلِيْ صَاحِبٌ مِنْ دُوْنِهِمْ لَا يَخُوْنُنِيْ

إِذَا الْتَبَسَتْ كَفِّيْ بِهِ يَتَأَكَّلُ

I have a friend besides them who will not betray,
When my hand relies on him, he stays steadfast.

وَإِنِّيْ كَفَانِيْ فَقْدُ مَنْ لَيْسَ جَازِيًا

بِحُسْنٰى وَلَا فِيْ قُرْبِهِ مُتَعَلَّلُ

And losing one who does not repay kindness,
Whose friendship holds no charm, is not a loss.

ثَلَاثَةُ أَصْحَابٍ فُؤَادٌ مُشَيَّعٌ

وَأَبْيَضُ إِصْلِيْتٌ وَصَفْرَاءُ عَيْطَلُ

Three friends compensate for that loss: a brave heart,
A gleaming blade, and a polished, long, yellow bow.

هَتُوْفٌ مِنَ الْمُلْسِ الْمُتُوْنِ يَزِيْنُهَا

رَصائِعُ قَد نيطَت إِلَيها وَمِحمَلُ

A bow of flexible core, embellished with,
Thongs that have been skilfully attached and worn.

إذا زَلَّ عَنْهَا السَّهْمُ حَنَّتْ كَأَنَّهَا

مُرَزَّأَةٌ عَجْلَى تُرِنُّ وَتُعوِلُ

It groans when arrows leave, like a grieving wife,
Whose son and husband are no more.

وَأَغْدُوْ خَمِيْصَ الْبَطْنِ لا يَستَفِزُّنِيْ

إِلَى الزَّادِ حِرْصٌ أَوْ فُؤَادٌ مُوَكِّلُ

And I rise with a hungry belly, not bothered,
By greed for possessions or a dependent heart towards them.

وَلَسْتُ بِمِهْيَافٍ يُعَشِّيْ سَوَامَهُ

مُجَدَّعَةً سُقبَانَها وَهْيَ بُهَّلُ

And I am not a tick who feeds his mounts,
However, starves them while he's round and fat.

وَلا جُبَّأٍ أَكْهَى مُرِبٍّ بِعِرْسِهِ

يُطَالِعُهَا فِيْ شَأْنِهِ كَيْفَ يَفْعَلُ

I'm not a coward, timid with my wife,
Asking her how to play my part in life.

وَلا خَرِقٍ هَيْقٍ كَأَنَّ فُؤادَهُ

يَظَلُّ بِهِ المُكَّاءُ يَعْلُوْ وَيَسْفِلُ

Nor am I an anxious ostrich, as if I were a lark?
We're fluttering up and down within my heart.

وَلَا خَالِفٍ دَارِيَّةٍ مُتغَزِّلٍ

يَرُوْحُ وَيَغْدُوْ دَاهِنًا يَتَكَحَّلُ

And I am not a deceitful man, flirting with women,
who goes around perfumed and applies makeup day and night.

وَلَسْتُ بِعَلٍّ شَرُّهُ دُوْنَ خَيْرِهِ

أَلَفَّ إِذَا مَا رُعْتَهُ اهْتَاجَ أَعْزَلُ

And I am not a tick who gains more harm than good,
Exposed, feeble, only moved by fright.

وَلَسْتُ بِمِحْيَارِ الظَّلَامِ إِذَا انْتَحَتْ

هُدَى الْهَوْجَلِ الْعِسِّيْفِ يَهْمَاءُ هَوْجَلُ

I am not afraid of the darkness, when the wild beasts roam,
In addition, the harsh cries of the lionesses resound.

إِذَا الْأَمْعَزُ الصَّوَّانُ لَاقٰى مَنَاسِمِيْ
تَطَايَرَ مِنْهُ قَادِحٌ وَمُفَلَّلُ

When the hard flint-stones meet my calloused feet,
Sparks fly up from them, and chips go flying.

أُدِيْمُ مِطَالَ الْجُوْعِ حَتّٰى أُمِيْتَهُ
وَأَضْرِبُ عَنْهُ الذِّكْرَ صَفحًا فَأَذْهَلُ

I endure the pangs of hunger till it dies,
And I push away the thought of it and forget.

وَأَسْتَفُّ تُرْبَ الْأَرْضِ كَيْلَا يَرٰى لَهُ
عَلَيَّ مِنَ الطَّوْلِ امْرُؤٌ مُتَطَوَّلُ

And I eat dust from the earth so that no one thinks,
I owe him anything. In addition, it appears to others, due to my height, that I am a long and stretched-out man.

وَلَوْلَا اجْتِنَابُ الذَّمِّ لَمْ يُلْفَ مَشْرَبٌ
يُعَاشُ بِهِ إِلَّا لَدَيَّ وَمَأْكَلُ

If I were not avoiding blame,
I would only have food and drink with me to live well,

وَلٰكِنَّ نَفْسًا مُرَّةً لَا تُقِيْمُ بِيْ

عَلٰى الذَّامِّ إِلَّا رَيْثَمَا أَتَحَوَّلُ

However, my restless soul does not remain at peace as long as it is blamed,

and I cannot find peace until I escape from it.

وَأَطْوِيْ عَلٰى الْخُمْصِ الْحَوَايَا كَمَا انْطَوَتْ

خُيُوْطَةُ مارِيٍّ تُغَارُ وَتُفْتَلُ

And I told my loins upon my hunger, as a seamstress folds,

The threads, that twist and turn and fight.

وَأُعْدِمُ أَحْيَانًا وَأَغْنٰى وَإِنَّمَا

يَنَالُ الْغِنٰى ذُو الْبُعَدَةِ الْمُتَبَذِّلُ

And sometimes I am poor and sometimes I am rich,

for wealth is attained by the diligent who strives for it.

فَلا جَزِعٌ مِنْ خَلَّةٍ مُتَكَشِّفٌ

وَلَا مَرِحٌ تَحْتَ الْغِنٰى أَتَخَيَّلُ

Therefore, I do not let poverty distress me,

Nor do I become arrogant in times of prosperity.

As we can see, Shanfarā possessed an intense sense of pride and independence. He was not interested in relying on others for his livelihood and preferred to live a simple and austere life, even if it meant enduring hunger and hardship. He valued loyalty and harboured a deep appreciation for nature and the beauty of the world surrounding him, as seen in his vivid descriptions of the landscape. These values are consistent with the most noble traditional Arab societal norms in Jāhiliyyah, translating smoothly into Islām and placing significant importance on self-sufficiency, honour, and a strong work ethic. It further promoted a view on masculinity that emphasised a sense of dignity and self-respect. Overall, the poem reflects traditional Arab cultural values and offers a timeless message of self-reliance and perseverance still relevant today.

ʿAbdullāh ibn Khāzim

ʿAbdullāh ibn Khāzim was a pre-Islāmic Arab poet from the tribe of Banū Sulaym. Despite his Arab lineage, ʿAbdullāh ibn Khāzim was noted to be black. Not much is known about his life or background, however his poetry has been admired for its eloquence and vivid imagery, often reflecting the harsh realities of life in the Arabian desert. His deep love for his tribe and his people was revealed through his poetry, as well as his pride in his Arab heritage.

Hammām ibn Muṭarraf

Hammām ibn Muṭarraf was another celebrated Black pre-Islāmic Arab poet from the tribe of Taghlib. He attained fame and recognition for his eloquent and powerful poetry that explored a range of themes including love, chivalry, and tribal life. Hammām's poetry was skilled at expressing complex emotions, mainly associated with the pain of separation from a loved one and the longing for their return. He also wrote extensively about the virtues of chivalry and the importance of keeping tribal allegiances and honour. In addition to his poetry, Hammām was known for his quick wit and sharp tongue. He was fearless in speaking his mind, even when it meant challenging social norms and cultural expectations. His bold and unapologetic style won him many admirers from poets to laypeople alike.

ʿAbdah ibn Ṭayyib

ʿAbdah ibn Ṭayyib was a renowned Black poet of the pre-Islāmic era who converted to Islām during the lifetime of the Prophet Muḥammad ﷺ. He was widely regarded as a talented poet, both before and after his conversion to Islām. His poetry was highly respected by classical Arabs, who considered it mandatory for any member of Arab high society to memorise a part of his works. This tradition of memorising his poems was also carried out by anyone who looked to be considered well-educated or erudite in Arabic culture. One of 'Abdah's most notable poems addressed the second Caliph, 'Umar ibn Al-Khaṭṭāb. Although much of 'Abdah's poetry and personal details have been lost to time, the few surviving poems offer us a glimpse into the depth of his talent and the esteem in which he was held by his contemporaries.

Suḥaym, the *Mawlā* of Banī Ḥasḥās

Suḥaym, also known as Habba, was a renowned Nubian poet who lived during the time of the Prophet Muḥammad ﷺ. He was originally an enslaved man, bought by 'Abdullāh ibn Abī Rabī'ah, who recognised Suḥaym's exceptional poetic talent and presented him as a gift to Caliph 'Uthmān ibn 'Affān. When 'Uthmān declined the gift, Suḥaym was bought and freed by the Banī Ḥasḥās tribe and became their mawlā (client).

One of Suḥaym's poems was quoted by the Prophet ﷺ and Abū Bakr, in which he said, "Old age and Islām are enough to forbid a person (from unfavourable actions)." During the time of 'Umar ibn Al-Khaṭṭāb, Suḥaym was brought before him to recite this poem, and upon finishing, 'Umar replied, "If you had mentioned Islām before old age, I would have rewarded you."

Another one of Suḥaym's poems was recited for the Prophet ﷺ, and the Prophet ﷺ proclaimed the author of this poem to be one of the people of Paradise, saying, "How true and excellent."

Suḥaym was particularly renowned for his love poems, which he wrote to many women he loved and admired from a distance: "Umairah', 'Ghāliyah', 'Hind', 'Asmā'", and 'Sulaymah', each loved and inaccessible due to his slave status. The subjects of his love poetry have since become archetypes in Arabic love poetry and are often referenced in both mystical and romantic works. Suḥaym's poems were unabashedly sensual and sometimes explicit, yet they also dealt with blackness, bondage, and the poor condition of Late Antique Arab society.

Faḍl al-Lahbī

Faḍl al-Lahbī was a prominent poet and relative of the Prophet Muḥammad ﷺ, who was also mentioned in the book "Al-Shuʿarāȧ as-Sūd wa Khasāʾiṣuhum fī ish-Shiʿri il-ʿArabī" by Professor Abduh. His father, ʿAbbās, was the grandson of Abū Lahab, who was the famous uncle and enemy of the Prophet ﷺ. His mother Āminah was the daughter of ʿAbbās ibn ʿAbdul Muṭṭalib, another paternal uncle of the Prophet ﷺ. Faḍl's grandfather, ʿUtbah ibn Abī Lahab, was married to Ruqayyah, the daughter of the Prophet ﷺ, before they divorced. Due to the animosity and hatred Abū Lahab (ʿUtbah's father) had for the Prophet ﷺ, ʿUtbah was made to divorce Ruqayyah and she later went on to marry ʿUthmān ibn ʿAffān. ʿUtbah accepted Islām during the conquest of Makkah. Both his son, ʿAbbās, and his grandson, Faḍl, were amongst the most talented poets of the Quraysh tribe. Faḍl was known for his dark complexion, earning him the nickname, 'The Green One'.

He took pride in his dark skin and authored a famous poem about it, in which he said:

وأَنَا الأَخْضَرُ مَنْ يَعْرِفْنِيْ

أَخْضَرُ الجِلْدَةِ فِيْ بَيْتِ الْعَرَبْ

"And I am The Green One, whoever knows me,
Knows I am the darkest skinned in all the houses of the Arabs."

Faḍl al-Lahbī's parents were of noble Qurayshī Arab descent. Some later commentators have suggested that his dark complexion may have come from an Ethiopian grandmother on his mother's side. However, there is limited information available about the identity of Āminah bint ʿAbbās' mother. As for Faḍl's paternal grandmother, she came from Yemen, so his dark complexion could have easily reflected the colour of South Arabians at that time, as opposed to some foreign ancestry.

Faḍl and his father ʿAbbās both lived in Makkah and later moved to Madīnah during the caliphate of ʿUthmān ibn ʿAffan. After ʿUthmān's death, they supported their relative, ʿAlī ibn Abī Ṭālib, during the civil wars against Muʿāwiyah and fought alongside him in the battles of Jamal and Ṣiffīn. During this time, Faḍl wrote several of his most notable poems against Muʿāwiyah and ʿAmr ibn ʿĀṣ. Despite ʿAlī's defeat, Faḍl kept cordial relationships with Muʿāwiyah and his successors, including ʿAbdul Malik ibn Marwān and his son Al-Walīd ibn ʿAbdul Malik, with whom he was close. Faḍl was even the first Hāshimī to praise an Ummayad in poetry after the wars between them.

These 'Crows of the Arabs' made significant contributions to pre-Islāmic Arabian society and culture. Through their artistry, they played a significant role in shaping the society that eventually gave rise to Islām and left an indelible mark on Arabic literature, still witnessed today. These Black poets, many of whom are of African heritage, offer a unique perspective on the complex connections between Africa and the Arab world and how they have shaped each other. While this chapter covers only a fraction of the Black poets who changed Arabian society and culture, this small selection shows their critical place in Arabic literature. Through studying their works, we gain a deeper understanding of the context and background of pre-Islāmic Arabia and the role of black figures in shaping the very environment that brought forth the miracle of the Prophet ﷺ, the Qur'ān.

It is worth noting that many of these poets were Arabs with East African mothers, which raises questions about the nature of the relationship between East Africa and the Arab world and the presence of these East African individuals in the Arabian Peninsula. Our ingrained notion of Africans being naturally enslaved or always bound to a state of enslavement blinds us to the fact that the Black presence in the Arabian Peninsula predates the Arab and Transatlantic slave trades. By examining this ancient link between Arabia and East Africa, we will gain a deeper understanding of the rich and diverse history of the Black community in the Arab world and how it shaped the region.

Chapter 2:

ḤABASH

Any reading of the biography of the Prophet Muḥammad ﷺ will unceasingly bring you to East Africa. We know, for instance, that the Prophet ﷺ describes himself as the descendant of an African woman, Hājar, the wife of the Prophet Ibrāhim and the founder of the city of Makkah, whose people, according to a narration in the Sīrah (prophetic biography) of Ibn Hishām, were 'of black skin and curly hair'.The Prophet ﷺ was born in the year of the elephant, which was when the Ethiopian general, Abrahah, marched on the Ka'bah. In his early life, after the death of his mother Āminah, the Prophet ﷺ was raised by Umm Ayman, also known as Barakah, who was an Ethiopian woman he lovingly always referred to as 'his mother after his mother'. Furthermore, when the Prophet ﷺ was given prophethood, he sent his early community to seek refuge with the Emperor of Axum, Najāshī. Over 80 companions of the Prophet ﷺ moved to

Axum, situated in present-day Ethiopia and Eritrea, and set up the first freely practising Muslim community. This made East Africa the first home of Islām.

The question arises; how did all these East Africans end up on the Arabian Peninsula in the first place? What was the relationship between East Africa and the Arab world? How did Abrahah end up becoming a ruler in South Yemen, and what was the reason for such a strong presence and familiarity with East Africa amongst the Arabs? These are the questions we will explore in this chapter.

Ḥabash

As Muslims, many of us grew up hearing the story of Najāshī, the emperor of Axum who gave Muslims refuge. He played a key role in the early history of Islām and has received much attention in different renditions of the Sīrah (prophetic biography), from being depicted in movies such as 'The Message' (released in 1976) to receiving much praise and acclaim in the books of early periods of the Sīrah. However, there is another little-known emperor of Axum who preceded him and had a significant impact on the Arabian Peninsula.

Saint Kaleb, a revered figure in Ethiopian history, is considered one of the great Ethiopian Emperors of the Axumite Empire. The stories of Kaleb's reign and his impact on the region have been passed down through generations and preserved in books such as the Kebra Nagast (the national epic of Ethiopia), recognising him as a significant figure in the history and culture of the nation. He reigned in the early 6th century AD and is known for his military conquests and expansion of the Axumite Empire. Kaleb's reign marked a period of prosperity and stability for Axum and he is remembered as a great leader and defender of the Christian faith.

Saint Kaleb is regarded as a saint in Ethiopian Orthodox Christianity for his role in spreading the faith and his devotion to God. According to tradition, he was a pious man who lived a life dedicated to the worship of God and the care of his people. He is said to have performed many miracles during his lifetime, including healing the sick, feeding the hungry, and converting many nonbelievers to faith. It is also believed that he was martyred for his beliefs and that his death was a testament to his unwavering devotion to God. These acts of piety and devotion, combined with the many miracles attributed to him, led to his canonisation as a saint by the Ethiopian Orthodox Church. Over time, Saint Kaleb became a symbol of faith and inspiration for many Ethiopian Christians, and his legacy continues to influence the Ethiopian Orthodox Church.

It was Kaleb's unwavering devotion to his faith that led him to respond to the calls of the Christians of Najrān in 525 AD. Najrān was a province found in the southern region of what is now Yemen and Saudi Arabia. It was home to a large population of East African and native Arab Christians. This diverse community existed even until the time of the Prophet Muḥammad ﷺ. In 631 AD, corresponding to the year 10 AH in the Islāmic calendar, the Prophet ﷺ began preaching the message of Islām and sent delegations to the leaders of neighbouring tribes and cities, including Najrān, inviting them to embrace Islām. The Christians of Najrān responded by sending a delegation to Madīnah to meet with the Prophet ﷺ and discuss their beliefs. The Treaty of Najrān, which resulted from this meeting, was characterised by respect and tolerance of each other's faiths. Both sides engaged in open and honest dialogue about their beliefs, and the Christians ultimately chose not to embrace Islām, agreeing to live in peace with the Muslims and pay the jizyah tax in exchange for protection. This treaty serves as a model for interreligious harmony and understanding.

Prior to the arrival of Islām, however, the situation was vastly different for the Christians of Najrān. They were subjected to persecution by the local ruler, Dhū Nuwās, and the persecution was so severe that they were even burned alive, as recounted in verses 4-10 of Sūrah al-Burūj, in the Qur'ān;

قُتِلَ أَصْحَٰبُ ٱلْأُخْدُودِ

Condemned are the makers of the ditch—

ٱلنَّارِ ذَاتِ ٱلْوَقُودِ

the fire ˹pit˺, filled with fuel—

إِذْ هُمْ عَلَيْهَا قُعُودٌ

when they sat around it,

وَهُمْ عَلَىٰ مَا يَفْعَلُونَ بِٱلْمُؤْمِنِينَ شُهُودٌ

watching what they had ˹ordered to be˺ done to the believers,

وَمَا نَقَمُوا۟ مِنْهُمْ إِلَّآ أَن يُؤْمِنُوا۟ بِٱللَّهِ ٱلْعَزِيزِ ٱلْحَمِيدِ

who they resented for no reason other than belief in Allah—the Almighty, the Praiseworthy—

ٱلَّذِى لَهُۥ مُلْكُ ٱلسَّمَـٰوَٰتِ وَٱلْأَرْضِ ۚ وَٱللَّهُ عَلَىٰ كُلِّ شَىْءٍ شَهِيدٌ

˹the One˺ to Whom belongs the kingdom of the heavens and earth. And Allah is a Witness over all things.

إِنَّ ٱلَّذِينَ فَتَنُوا۟ ٱلْمُؤْمِنِينَ وَٱلْمُؤْمِنَـٰتِ ثُمَّ لَمْ يَتُوبُوا۟ فَلَهُمْ عَذَابُ جَهَنَّمَ
وَلَهُمْ عَذَابُ ٱلْحَرِيقِ

Those who persecute the believing men and women and then do not repent will certainly suffer the punishment of Hell and the torment of burning.

إِنَّ ٱلَّذِينَ ءَامَنُوا۟ وَعَمِلُوا۟ ٱلصَّٰلِحَٰتِ لَهُمْ جَنَّٰتٌ تَجْرِى مِن تَحْتِهَا ٱلْأَنْهَٰرُ ۚ ذَٰلِكَ ٱلْفَوْزُ ٱلْكَبِيرُ

Surely those who believe and do good will have Gardens under which rivers flow. That is the greatest triumph.

The oppressors in these verses are described as "makers of the ditch—the fire pit, filled with fuel" who "sat around it, watching what they had ordered to be done to the believers." During that period of severe persecution, the Christians of Najrān, sought refuge with Kaleb, much like the early Muslim community sought refuge with Kaleb's successor, Najāshī. Kaleb, moved by their pleas, assembled a large army and marched towards Arabia to put an end to the persecution. He defeated Dhū Nuwās in battle and set up his rule over the region, bringing an end to the oppression of the Christians of Najrān. This act of bravery and protection of the oppressed earned Kaleb a great deal of respect and admiration among the Christians of Najrān and the surrounding areas. This act also solidified his legacy as a just and fair ruler who stood up for those who were being mistreated.

Both Ibn Kathīr and Ibn Hishām, amongst others, mention the story of Saint Kaleb and his invasion of Arabia in their respective historical texts, 'Al-Bidāyah wa an-Nihāyah' and 'As-Sīrah an-Nabawiyyah'. Kaleb's reign was one of the first instances of strong African power in the region, marking a significant moment in the history of the

Arabian Peninsula. The presence of Ethiopian Christians and their interactions with the Arabian communities helped usher in an era of more widespread Abrahamic faith in Southern Arabia, setting the stage for the later rise of Islām.

During this campaign, Kaleb's general was Abrahah, who is also known for his infamous invasion of Makkah with an army of elephants, as mentioned in Sūrah al-Fīl in the Qur'ān. After King Kaleb's forces defeated Dhū Nuwās, Abrahah was appointed as the viceroy of South Arabia. However, Abrahah soon declared himself the independent King of Ḥimyar and set up his rule over the region. This act of rebellion earned Abrahah the wrath of King Kaleb, who sent his general 'Āriyah to take over the governorship of Yemen.

There are different accounts of what happened next. According to some accounts, Abrahah fought a duel with 'Āriyah, which resulted in 'Āriyah's death and Abrahah suffering a facial injury that earned him the sobriquet 'scar-face'. Nevertheless, Abrahah was able to keep his grip on power and gain formal recognition from King Kaleb's successor in return for nominal tribute.

Abrahah then went on to become a prominent figure in Yemenī history, known for his efforts to spread Christianity in Central Arabia. Abrahah constructed the Al-Qalīs Church in Ṣan'ā'. The word 'Al-Qalīs' has its roots in the Greek word 'Ekklesia', meaning 'an assembly or congregation'. It is believed that this was the cathedral built by Abrahah to rival the Kaʿbah in Makkah. Abrahah also built churches in Najrān for Banī Al-Ḥārith, in Ṭā'if for the tribe of Thaqīf, and in Yemen for the tribes of Yarīm and Ghamdān.

Abrahah's reign was documented through inscriptions on the Mārib Dam, recording his suppression of a rebellion led by Esimiphaios', the former king of Ḥimyar's son and his repairs to the dam. He received envoys from the Negus, Byzantium, Persia, and Al-Ḥārith ibn Jabalah, the phylarch of Arabia, and celebrated the completion of the repairs with a grand feast. Following his successes, Abrahah adopted the royal title of 'King of Sabaʿ, Dhū-Raydān, Haḍramawt, Yamanat, and their Arabs on the plateau and the lowland', which was previously used by the Ḥimyarites. This title reflected his authority over the region and solidified his position as a powerful ruler in Yemen.

We can see that the Arabian Peninsula, prior to the advent of Islām, was characterised by its rich cultural and ethnic diversity. Interregional relationships played a crucial role in shaping the history and identity of the region, with the ancient Kingdom of Axum and the Kingdom of Ḥimyar having a significant impact on the area. The close ties between the two regions, eased by trade and exchange, led to a diverse community of East Africans living in the Arabian Peninsula. The fact that the majority of these East

Africans were free people rather than enslaved is a testament to the respect and trust that existed between the two communities. Their histories and influence were so great on the Arabs that their stories even warranted being mentioned in the Qur'ān itself.

As previously mentioned, the deep-rooted relationship between the Arabian Peninsula and East Africa is clear in the early days of Islām and the life of the Prophet Muḥammad ﷺ. It must be remembered that the first hijrah (migration) was not the prophetic migration to Madīnah but took place several years prior. A small group of companions, including the Prophet's daughter, Ruqayyah, her husband 'Uthmān, who was the Prophet's third successor, the Prophet's cousin Ja'far ibn Abī Ṭālib, along with Sa'd ibn Abī Waqās, Zubayr ibn 'Awwām and 'Abdur Raḥmān ibn 'Awf, crossed the Red Sea upon the advice of the Prophet ﷺ himself to seek refuge in the ancient East African Empire of Axum. The Prophet ﷺ recommended them, "If you were to go to Abyssinia [it would be better for you], for the king will not tolerate injustice and it is a friendly country, until such a time as Allāh shall relieve you from your distress."

Upon their arrival, they were received admirably by King Najāshī. They were defended by him upon the arrival of a delegation sent by the Quraysh to disrupt their migration and take them back to Arabia. They lived in peace, free to openly practise Islām without fear of oppression or persecution, until the Prophet ﷺ established Madīnah and they were able to return to him in Arabia. Najāshī went on to convert to Islām and develop a close relationship with the Prophet ﷺ. The Prophet ﷺ also trusted him and made him his representative when he married Umm Ḥabībah, who was living in Ethiopia at the time. The Prophet ﷺ held him in high esteem, and Saʿīd ibn Al-Musayyib reported that upon the authority of Abū Hurayrah, "The Messenger of Allāh ﷺ announced the passing of Al-Najāshī on the day wherein he died. Thus, he went out to the muṣallā (place of prayer) and ordered his companions to stand in rows behind him. He performed the funeral prayer for him, making the takbīr (proclamation of the greatness of God) on him four times."

The significance of the first hijrah cannot be overstated. The first place to accept Islām, the first place where Islām was openly practised, and the first free Muslim community was set up, not in Arabia, as many would presume, but in Africa. Furthermore, not only was Africa Islām's first welcoming home, but the Prophet ﷺ himself, while living in Arabia, was surrounded by Africans and Black Arabs before and after the hijrah to Madīnah. Many of them played major roles in the formation of the Early Muslim community; contributions that, over time, seem to have been forgotten or overlooked.

The relationship between the Prophet ﷺ and the kingdom of Axum was marked by mutual respect and hospitality. This is evident in the narrations of Abū Qatādah, Ibn Isḥāq, and Ibn Hishām in their biographies of the Prophet ﷺ. They record that when King Najāshī sent a delegation to Madīnah, the Prophet ﷺ honoured and served the visitors himself, despite the protests of his companions who offered to serve the delegation instead. The Prophet ﷺ insisted on serving them as a show of respect for King Najāshī's support and hospitality towards the Muslims.

One of the gifts that the Prophet ﷺ received from Najāshī was a pair of pure black leather socks. These were brought to him by the companion, 'Amr ibn Umayyah, and held a special place in the Prophet's heart. He would often wear these socks as a symbol of his gratitude for the kindness of the Abyssinians. Another important gift that the Prophet ﷺ received from Abyssinia was a signet ring. This ring was crafted in 6 AH after the Treaty of Ḥudaybiyyah by Ya'lā ibn Umayyah in Madīnah. It was made of silver and had an Abyssinian gemstone - which was either made of onyx or agate - on it. The Prophet ﷺ would use this ring to seal official correspondence with the kings of his time. Ibn Ḥajar mentions in his commentary on the Hadith about this ring, that the stone was extracted from the soil of Abyssinia, and was brought to the Hijaz from Abyssinia, and the ring was crafted by an Abyssinian.

The signet ring held great significance to the Prophet ﷺ and his successors. After his passing, the later Caliphs,

Abū Bakr, 'Umar and 'Uthmān, all used this ring for their correspondences. Unfortunately, the ring was lost in 30 AH, during the reign of 'Uthmān, when it fell into the well of Arīs outside of Madīnah. It was never found again, despite the search for the ring lasting three days. Some scholars believe this marked the beginning of tribulations in the Islāmic world, which continue to this day.

Finally, Najāshī sent the Abyssinian tribe of Banū Arfidah to protect and serve the Prophet ﷺ and his noble family. This tribe was known to perform their traditional dances with shields and spears in utter joy at the coming of the Prophet ﷺ into Madīnah, such that on the days of 'Eīd, the Prophet ﷺ and his wife 'Ā'ishah (may Allāh be pleased with her) would watch their displays with delight. The Prophet ﷺ always showed kindness and respect to the Banū Arfidah, even when others rebuked them for their behaviour.

The Prophet ﷺ allowed them to sing and dance, praise Allāh and His Messenger in their native language, and the Messenger of Allāh ﷺ appreciated the displays of devotion offered through the framework of their heritage and culture, a sunnah that is often neglected in today's world. Remarkably, the Prophet ﷺ never required these Black and African converts of Islām to abandon their tradition, nor did he force them to Arabize themselves to be considered true, upright Muslims. This serves as an important lesson for modern Muslims; we must always strive to keep that same level of respect and appreciation as the Prophet ﷺ for the diverse cultures and backgrounds that inhabit our present Muslim community.

Prophet Muḥammad ﷺ was not only surrounded by Africans in Arabia, but the influence of East Africa can also be seen around him, namely in the language of the Qur'ān. Many scholars of tafsīr (exegesis of the Qur'ān) have pointed out that several words in the Qur'ān have their origins in the Habesha language. In Raf'u Shȧni il-Ḥabshān by Imām al-Suyūṭī, he produces an entire chapter on the topic, building off the authority of the Qur'ānic scholar, Ibn al-Jawzī. Within the chapter, he then offered a few examples of the words and expressions belonging to said origin, some of which I shall reproduce here.

Regarding His (Almighty) words:

فَوَلِّ وَجْهَكَ شَطْرَ الْمَسْجِدِ الْحَرَامِ ۚ

So, turn your face towards the Sacred Mosque

[Qur'ān 2:144]

Rāfi' said that the word translated as 'towards' (shaṭra) means 'in its direction' in Ethiopian.

With the same chain of transmission to Ibn Abī Ḥātim, who said, "It was mentioned on the authority of Nu'aym ibn Ḥammād al-Miṣrī, who narrated from'Abdul Ḥamīd ibn 'Abdir Raḥmān al-Ḥimmānī, who narrated to us on the authority of An-Naḍr Abū ʿUmar, on the authority of ʿIkrimah, that regarding His (Allāh's) words:

يُؤْمِنُونَ بِالْجِبْتِ وَالطَّٰغُوتِ

They believe in Jibt (idols) and false gods.

[Qurʾān 4:51]

Ibn ʿAbbās said, "ʿAl-Jibt' is a name of Satan in Ethiopian."

Regarding His (Exalted is He) words:

إِنَّ إِبْرَٰهِيمَ لَأَوَّٰهٌ حَلِيمٌ

Abraham was truly awwāh (tender-hearted), forbearing.

[Qurʾān 9:114]

Mujāhid and ʿIkrimah both said, "ʿAl-Awwāh' means ʿspiritually certain' in Ethiopic. ʿAmr ibn Shurāhbil said, "ʿAl-Awwāh' means ʿconstantly merciful' in Ethiopic." Ibn ʿAbbās said, "ʿAl-Awwāh' means ʿspiritually certain' in Ethiopic." Muḥammad ibn Saʿd related, from his father, who narrated from his uncle, on the authority of his grandfather, that Ibn ʿAbbās said about His words,"ʿAl-Awwāh' means ʿbeliever' in Ethiopic."

Regarding His (Almighty) words:

فَلَمَّا سَمِعَتْ بِمَكْرِهِنَّ أَرْسَلَتْ إِلَيْهِنَّ وَأَعْتَدَتْ لَهُنَّ مُتَّكَـًٔا

When she heard about their gossip, she invited them and set a banquet for them.

[Qur᾿ān 12:31]

ʻAbdullāh al-Shaqrī said, "The word translated as 'banquet' (muttakaan) in Ethiopian is a grapefruit." This was narrated by Abū ul-Shaykh ibn Ḥayyān in his Qur'ānic Commentary (Tafsīr).

Regarding His (Almighty) words:

ٱلَّذِينَ ءَامَنُوا۟ وَعَمِلُوا۟ ٱلصَّـٰلِحَـٰتِ طُوبَىٰ لَهُمْ وَحُسْنُ مَـَٔابٍ

Those who believe and do good, for them will be bliss and an honourable destination.

[Qur᾿ān 13:29]

Ibn ʻAbbās said, "The word translated as bliss (ṭūbā) is a name for Paradise in Ethiopian."

Saʻīd said, "The word 'Ṭūbā' is a name for Paradise in Ethiopian."

Regarding His (Almighty) word:

طه

Ṭā Hā

[Qur᾿ān 20:1]

Ibn ʿAbbās said, "It is like 'Oh Muḥammad!' in Ethiopian." Al-Ḥākim said, "Its chain of transmission is authentic."

ʿUmar ibn Abī Zā'idah narrated, "I heard ʿIkrimah saying, 'Ṭā Hā' means, "Oh Man!" in Ethiopian."

Regarding His (Almighty) words:

ٱللَّهُ نُورُ ٱلسَّمَٰوَٰتِ وَٱلْأَرْضِ ۚ مَثَلُ نُورِهِۦ كَمِشْكَوٰةٍ فِيهَا مِصْبَاحٌ

Allāh is the Light of the heavens and the earth. His light is like a niche in which there is a lamp...

[Qurʾān 24:35]

Saʿd ibn ʿIyāḍ ath-Thumālī said "The word translated as 'lamp' (al-Mishkāt) is a 'kuwwah' in Ethiopian. Kuwwah is an opening or a narrow slit in a wall. It is also said that it is a dome-like structure on a roof that enables side openings for ventilation.

Regarding His (Almighty) words:

يَٰٓأَيُّهَا ٱلَّذِينَ ءَامَنُوا۟ ٱتَّقُوا۟ ٱللَّهَ وَءَامِنُوا۟ بِرَسُولِهِۦ يُؤْتِكُمْ كِفْلَيْنِ مِن رَّحْمَتِهِۦ

O people of faith! Fear Allāh and believe in His Messenger. ⸢And⸣ He will grant you a double share of His mercy

[Qurʾān 57:28]

Abū Mūsā al-Ashʿarī said "The word translated as 'double share' (Kiflayn) means 'double' in Ethiopian.

Regarding His (Almighty) words:

إِنَّ نَاشِئَةَ اللَّيْلِ هِىَ أَشَدُّ وَطْـًٔا وَأَقْوَمُ قِيْلًا

Indeed, worship at night is more impactful and suitable for recitation.

[Qurʾān 73:6]

Ibn ʿAbbās said, "The word that comes before night and is translated as 'worship' (nashʾah) in Ethiopian means to 'stand'"

Regarding this verse, ʿAbdullāh said, "It (nāshiʾah), in Ethiopian, refers to the night vigil prayers." Al-Ḥākim said, "Its chain of narration is authentic."

Saʿīd ibn Jubayr said about this verse, "It means when someone keeps prayer vigil a part of the night. In Ethiopian, 'So and so nashảa' means that they kept prayer vigil a part of the night."

Regarding His (Almighty) word:

يٰسٓ

Yāsīn

[Qurʾān 36:1]

Ibn ʿAbbās said, "It means, 'Oh Human Being!' in Ethiopian."

Regarding His (Almighty) words:

يَوْمَ نَطْوِى السَّمَآءَ كَطَيِّ السِّجِلِّ لِلْكُتُبِ

On that Day We will roll up the sky like the sijill rolls up scrolls...

[Qurʾān 21:104]

Ibn ʿAbbās said, "A sijill, in Ethiopian means 'man'."

Regarding His (Almighty) words:

وَمِنْ ثَمَرَٰتِ النَّخِيْلِ وَالْأَعْنٰبِ تَتَّخِذُوْنَ مِنْهُ سَكَرًا وَرِزْقًا حَسَنًا

And from the fruits of palm trees and grapevines you derive intoxicants and a wholesome provision.

[Qurʾān 16:67]

Ibn ʿAbbās said, "the word translated as 'intoxicant' (sakar) in Ethiopian means vinegar."

Regarding His (Almighty) words:

وَقِيْلَ يٰٓأَرْضُ ابْلَعِيْ مَآءَكِ

And it was said to the Earth, swallow your water

[Qurʾān 11:44]

Wahb ibn Munabbih said, "In Ethiopian, the word 'swallow' (ibliʿī) means "Swallow."

Regarding His (Almighty) words:

لَا جَرَمَ أَنَّهُمْ فِى الْآخِرَةِ هُمُ الْأَخْسَرُوْنَ

Without a doubt, they will be the worst losers in the Hereafter.

[Qurʾān 11:22]

ʿIkrimah said, "The word translated as 'without a doubt' (jarama) means 'obligated' in Ethiopian."

Regarding His (Almighty) words:

إِنَّكُمْ وَمَا تَعْبُدُوْنَ مِنْ دُوْنِ اللهِ حَصَبُ جَهَنَّمَ أَنْتُمْ لَهَا وٰرِدُوْنَ

Certainly, you ˹disbelievers˺ and whatever you worship instead of Allāh will be the fuel of Hell. You are ˹all˺ bound to enter it.

[Qurʾān 21:98]

Ibn ʿAbbās said ,"The word translated as 'fuel' (ḥaṣab) means 'the firewood of hell' in the Zanjī language.

The term Zanjī is derived from Zanj, a name used by mediaeval Muslim geographers to refer to both a certain part of Southeast Africa (primarily the Swāḥilī Coast) and its Bantu inhabitants. This word is also the origin of the name Zanzibar ('coast of the Zanj') and the Sea of Zanj (Western Indian Ocean). In Lisān al-ʿArab, they are defined as a tribe of black people that live along the Equator, their lands stretching from the Western coast of Africa to the lands of Ethiopia. However, the inhabitants of that area include a vast number of tribes with different languages.

Regarding His (Almighty) words:

وَطُوْرِ سِيْنِيْنَ

And (by the oath of) Mount Sinai

[Qurʾān 95:2]

ʿIkrimah said, "And Mount Sīnīn, that 'Sīnīn' means 'beautiful' in Ethiopian.

Nāfiʿ ibn Al-Azraq said to Ibn ʿAbbās, "Inform me about the words of God Almighty:

إِنَّهُ ظَنَّ أَن لَّن يَّحُوْرَ

Truly he thought he would never return.

[Qurʾān 84:14]

He said, "the word translated as 'return' (yaḥūru) means 'to return' in Ethiopian."

The Prophet ﷺ also used words from the Ethiopian language. It is narrated from Um Khālid bint Khālid:

"When I came from Ethiopia (to Madīnah), I was a young girl. Allāh's Messenger ﷺ made me wear a sheet with marks on it. Allāh's Messenger ﷺ was rubbing those marks with his hands saying, "Sanāh! Sanāh!", which means 'beautiful' in Ethiopia." [Ṣaḥīḥ al-Bukhārī #3874]

With the previous chain of narration to Imām Aḥmad, Yaḥyā narrated, on the authority of ʿUbayd ibn ʿIyāḍ ibn Laqīt narrated, "I heard my father mentioning that Ḥudhayfah said, "The Messenger of Allāh ﷺ was asked about the Last Hour. He said, "The knowledge of that is with my Nurturing Master. He does not reveal it to anyone apart from Himself. However, I will inform you of some of its signs and what will come before it. Before it will come trials and haraj." He was asked, "Oh Messenger of Allāh! We know what trials are. What is haraj?" He said, "It means killing in Ethiopian."" [Musnad Aḥmad]

This highlights the degree to which the cultural exchange between the two regions permeated the setting in which Islām developed. The movement between both cultures bore significant fruits not only in theological realms but also in linguistic realms. It is worth mentioning that even though the Arabs used the term 'Ḥabashi - which I have translated as Ethiopian or Ethiopic, there is no single language referred to as 'Ethiopian' or 'Ethiopic.' In Ethiopia today, there exist between 45 and 86 distinct languages, as reported by 'Translators without Borders.' The most widely spoken languages among the Ethiopian population include Oromo, Amharic, Tigrinya, Sidamo, and Afar. The origin of specific terms therefore is often unclear, and they may stem from various languages or even a mixture of dialects. Historically, due to a lack of precise knowledge, the term

'Ḥabashi' was used by Arabs as a general reference to the languages in the region.

If you are interested in delving deeper into the said subject exchange, from the Late Antique to the Medieval, I highly recommend reading 'Tanwīr al-Ghabash fī Faḍli il-Sudān wa al-Ḥabash' by Ibn Jawzī and 'Rafʿu Shȧni il-Ḥabshān' by Imām Suyūṭī, both written in the 11th and 14th centuries, respectively. The latter work has been beautifully translated by my brother, Imam Muhammad Adeyinka Mendes, under the title 'The Spirits of Black Folk: Sages Through the Ages'. Despite this subject being ignored or undervalued in the Muslim community, these scholars, who dedicated themselves to writing about the most important religious and secular sciences, saw fit to also write about the virtue of the Sudanese and Abyssinians. This is a testament to the high regard they held for the topic. Both aforementioned works highlight the importance of the relationship between the Prophet ﷺ and the people of East Africa and Ethiopia and are a testament to the serious regard with which this subject should be held.

Chapter 3:

ISLĀM IN EAST AFRICA

As pointed out by Abdulrahman Abdulkadri in his book review of Beyond Bilal for the Traversing Tradition website, the book focuses largely on the history of Islām in West Africa but gives only a brief overview of the Muslims of Eastern Africa, and a more in-depth exploration of the spread of Islām to regions such as Sudan, Ethiopia, Somalia, and the Swāḥilī coast would have added significant value to the book.

I chose not to delve into the history of Islām in East Africa in Beyond Bilal for several reasons. Firstly, I believe the history of Islām in East Africa has already been significantly emphasised in the Sīrah and most Islāmic discourse and it is often the only aspect of Black history in Islām that many people are acquainted with. Most people are familiar with events such as the first hijrah and the presence of East Africans in early Islām, which is in stark contrast to their lack of knowledge about Islām in West Africa, of which they know very little.

Secondly, I was not well-versed in the history of the spread of Islām in East Africa, and I would have preferred someone else with more ability and experience in the region to write about it. Finally, as a West African myself, I felt that it might have been inappropriate for me to encroach on that region and attempt to write its history when there are a plethora of capable and knowledgeable East African scholars, both young and old, who could do a much better job than I could.

Thirdly, I felt that the subject of the spread of Islām in East Africa was deserving of its own book, and so, after many requests from East Africans who attended my lectures across the USA, UK, Canada and from those who reached out to me on social media, I decided to respond to their requests through this book, In shā' Allāh. I hope that it can serve as an introduction to the subject and supply a comprehensive overview until more knowledgeable and experienced East African scholars can supply a more detailed account of the history.

The countries that make up East Africa include Sudan, South Sudan, Somalia, Kenya, Tanzania, Rwanda, Burundi, Uganda, and Ethiopia. In this chapter, we will examine the history of the spread of Islām in these regions, beginning with Sudan and moving south. Then, in the following chapters, we will explore how the people of these countries changed the wider Muslim world, including the Middle East and Asia.

Sudan

Other than claims that companions of the Prophet Muḥammad ﷺ sailed into Dongola in Sudan on their way to Axum during the first hijrah, there is limited evidence to support Islām being introduced to Sudan until the Islāmic conquest of Egypt led by ʿAmr ibn al-ʿĀs. Although there had been cultural exchange between Nubians and Arabs prior to the rise of Islām, the actual spread of Islām in Sudan was largely facilitated by the political and military conquests of the Arab armies, allowing Arab merchants and travellers to introduce Islām to the region.

Prior to the rise of Islām, the Nubian kingdoms of Nobatia, Makuria, and Alodia were found along the Nile River and had long-standing trade and cultural relationships with the neighbouring Arab tribes. The Nubians were known for their gold mines, and this valuable resource attracted Arab merchants who established trade routes between the Nubian kingdoms and the Arabian Peninsula.

Nubian civilisation is believed to have appeared around the 8th century BC and is renowned for its rich cultural and political history. It was home to and the origin of many powerful states, including the Kingdom of Kerma (circa

2500 BC - 1500 BC), the Kingdom of Kush (circa 1069 BC- 350 AD) and the Napatan dynasty (circa 751 BC - 300 AD).

Nubia and ancient Egypt maintained a complex relationship throughout history. At times, Nubia was a rival to ancient Egypt, while at other times, they formed alliances. During the New Kingdom period of ancient Egypt (circa 1570 BC - 1069 BC), Nubia became a vassal state of Egypt, leading to Nubian royalty being educated in Egypt and intermarrying with Egyptian royalty. Thereafter, the Nubian kingdom of Kush eventually gained independence from Egypt and went on to conquer and rule Egypt for a period, forming the 25th dynasty of Egypt, also known as the Nubian dynasty.

This dynasty saw the construction of several pyramids in Nubia. The Nubian pyramids were built in a similar style to the ancient Egyptian pyramids, with steep sides and a flat top, despite being typically smaller in size and lacking the characteristic of having a smooth exterior like that of the Egyptian pyramids.

The Nubian pyramids, while not as well-known as the Egyptian pyramids, are considered to be some of the most well-preserved pyramids in the world and are a testament to the Nubians' architectural prowess and their close connection to their ancient Egyptian neighbours. In fact, there are more pyramids in Sudan than in Egypt, all of which are believed to have been built between the 8th century BC and the 4th century AD as tombs for the Nubian elites.

In the period of Islāmic expansion after the death of the Prophet ﷺ, the Arabs - having successfully conquered Egypt under ʿAmr ibn al-ʿĀs (a companion of the Prophet ﷺ) - set their sights on Sudan. In 642 AD, ʿAmr ibn al-ʿĀs sent a column of 20,000 horsemen under his relative, ʿUqbah ibn Nāfiʿ, against Makuria with the intention of conquering the Nubian kingdom. The Arab forces made it as far as Dongola, the capital of Makuria, but were met with strong resistance from the Nubian forces. According to the historian Al-Balādhurī, the Nubians fought fiercely and showered the Arab forces with arrows, leading to a rare defeat for the Rāshidūn Caliphate. Many of the Arab forces were wounded and blinded due to the deadly accuracy of the Nubian archers. This event was marked as the first Battle of Dongola and, despite the Arab loss, delineates an important moment in the history of the region and the spread of Islām into Sudan.

In 651 AD, the Arabs tried once again. The Umayyad governor of Egypt, ʿAbdullāh ibn Saʿīd ibn Abī is-Sarḥ, led a force of 5,000 men to the Makurian capital, Dongola. His forces were equipped with heavy cavalry and a catapult, likely a traction trebuchet, which Al-Maqrīzī, a mediaeval Egyptian historian and biographer during the Mamlūk era who detailed the attempted Arab invasion of Nubia, stated the Makurians had never seen such a trebuchet before. ʿAbdullāh then laid siege to the city, placing his cavalry in the dangerous position of attacking a walled city defended by the renowned Nubian archers. During the siege, reports claim that the town's cathedral sustained damage from catapult fire, a claim that corresponds to the material evidence of a damaged church dating to the mid-seventh century AD being discovered outside the remains of the city walls.

The siege ultimately ended in a pitched battle. ʿAbdullāh's forces suffered heavy casualties, and King Qalidurut, the King of Makuria, did not sue for peace. In the end, ʿAbdullāh called off the siege and negotiated a pact known as 'the Baqṭ'. According to the 9th-century Egyptian historian, Ibn ʿAbdul Hakām, this was because ʿAbdullāh was stuck in a stalemate, "unable to defeat them." The 10th-century historian Aḥmad al-Kūfī, who held no sympathy for the caliphate's forces, offered a more poignant assessment, where he said "The Muslims had never [before] suffered a loss like the one they had in Nubia."

The Baqṭ treaty lasted for six centuries, making it - according to some reports - humanity's longest observed peace treaty. It marked one of the longest-standing diplomatic relationships between a Muslim and non-Muslim state, with Nubia still being free from Muslim conquest. This arrangement allowed Nubia to keep its Christian identity and set up trade relations with Muslim Egypt.

Under the terms of the treaty, both sides agreed to engage in mutually beneficial trade. The treaty also included provisions related to the protection of each other's borders, the safe passage of travellers and merchants, and the return of fugitives. Although it was not designed to directly promote the Islāmisation of Sudan, it played a leading role in the gradual diffusion of Islāmic culture, ideas, and practices into Nubian society.

The close relations between Nubians and Muslims led to intermarriages between the two communities over time, exposing Nubians to Islāmic culture and helping the adoption of the Islāmic faith. It is also possible some Nubians voluntarily converted to Islām for economic, political, or social advantages. Given the close relations with powerful Muslim states in the region, conversion to Islām would have offered Nubians better trade opportunities or alliances with their Muslim neighbours.

Over the centuries, the continuous interaction between Nubians and Muslims, coupled with cultural, social, and economic factors, led to the gradual assimilation of Islāmic customs and practices in Nubian society. The process of Islāmisation was likely a complex and multifaceted one, occurring over an extended period and involving various aspects of society. In the context of the Christian Nubian Kingdom, the Islāmisation process may have initially been slow and uneven, with pockets of Muslim communities primarily forming in urban centres and along trade routes. Despite this, as the political power of the Nubian Kingdom waned, the influence of Islāmic culture and religion grew stronger. The eventual decline of the Nubian Kingdom in the late 12th or early 13th century AD further contributed to the Islāmisation of the region. As the Nubian state disintegrated, Muslim states and tribes expanded their influence and control over Sudanese territory, bringing with them Islāmic law, administration, and education.

Thereafter, in 1504 AD, came the appearance of one of the most successful of the successor kingdoms, the Fūnj Sultanate. The Fūnj Sultanate appeared as a powerful Muslim state in the region, dominating northern Sudan and setting up its capital at Sennar. Under the Fūnj Sultanate, a centralised system of governance and administration based on Islāmic principles and Sharīʿah Law was introduced. This centralised rule allowed for the Fūnj Sultanate's authority and adherence to Islāmic traditions to become increasingly intertwined, encouraging the conversion to Islām amongst the Sudanese population.

Moreover, the Fūnj Sultanate actively promoted the construction of mosques, madrasahs (Islāmic schools), and other religious institutions. These establishments served as centres of learning and worship, playing a vital role in grassroots Islāmic missionary efforts. The support for religious institutions also attracted Islāmic scholars and teachers to the region, further contributing to the Islāmisation process. The Fūnj Sultanate pursued diplomatic relations and alliances with other prominent Islāmic states, further solidifying its ties to the broader Islāmic world. Through these relationships, the Sultanate gained access to resources, knowledge, and connections which helped strengthen its position as a Muslim power and enhanced the spread of Islām within its borders.

As the Fūnj Sultanate expanded its territory and influence over the centuries, the prevalence of Islām grew in the region. By the time the Sultanate's power began to wane in the early 19th century AD, Islām had become deeply rooted in Sudanese society. As for today, Sudan is overwhelmingly Muslim, with an estimated 97% of the population adhering to Islām.

South Sudan

The Islāmisation of South Sudan, on the other hand, was a different and more complex process compared to the rest of Sudan. The majority of South Sudan's population today adheres to Christianity and traditional African religions, with only a small minority practising Islām. The region's unique history and the prolonged conflict between the north and the south have played a significant role in shaping its religious landscape.

During the Ottoman and Anglo-Egyptian rule in

Sudan (from the 19th century AD until 1956), when what is now known as Sudan and South Sudan were administered as one nation, the northern Muslim elites tried to expand their influence in the southern region. However, British colonial policy aimed to keep the South separate from the Muslim-majority North. The British implemented a 'Southern Policy' to preserve the distinct cultural and religious identity of the South, limiting the spread of Islām and promoting Christian missionary activity.

When Sudan gained independence in 1956, the tensions between the north and the south escalated into a series of civil wars (1955-1972 and 1983-2005). The conflicts were driven not only by religious differences but also by political, economic, and ethnic factors. During these wars, the northern Sudanese government made extensive efforts to impose Islāmic law and the Arabic language on the entire country, including the largely non-Muslim south. These policies fuelled resentment amongst the southern population, leading to increased resistance against the north and the strengthening of their Christian and traditional African religious identities.

In 2005, the Comprehensive Peace Agreement (CPA) was signed, ending the civil war and paving the way for South Sudan's independence. The CPA granted the South autonomy in religious matters, allowing them to support their predominantly Christian and traditional African religious practices. South Sudan eventually gained independence in 2011, becoming the world's youngest nation. The long-lasting conflict and South Sudan's eventual independence have served to further solidify its religious affiliations, resulting in a more intricate and less extensive Islāmisation process when compared to the rest of Sudan. According to the CIA World Factbook, Muslims constitute a small minority in South Sudan, accounting for approximately 6% of the population.

Somalia

Before the advent of Islām in Somalia, the region was home to various ancient cultures and religions. One of the primary belief systems was the traditional Somali religion, which was centred around the worship of Wāq, who they viewed as a supreme sky deity. This belief system also revered ancestral spirits and natural elements, having various rituals and practices associated with it. Nonetheless, Wāqism was also largely a monotheistic faith that venerated Wāq. The Somali people have long been renowned for their rich oral tradition, with poetry and storytelling playing an essential role in preserving their cultural heritage and beliefs. Poets, or 'Abwān' in Somali, held a special place in society as the keepers of history, wisdom, and cultural identity. Somali oral literature encompasses various forms of poetry, including gabay (a form of didactic or philosophical verse), jiifto (satirical verse), and burānbur (a traditional women's verse form). These forms of poetry were often used to convey moral lessons, praise or criticise individuals, and express political opinions or emotions.

In pre-Islāmic times, the Somali region had connections with various ancient civilisations, such as Egyptians, Phoenicians, and Greeks. These connections further influenced the cultural landscape of pre-Islāmic Somalia. For instance, the ancient Egyptians referred to 'the Land of Punt', which many historians believe was in present-day Somalia or the broader Horn of Africa region. Punt was described as 'Ta Netjeru', meaning 'the Land of the Gods', and was a crucial trading partner of ancient Egypt. The Egyptians imported valuable commodities from punt, such as gold, frankincense, myrrh, and exotic animals.

The Phoenicians, a maritime civilisation that originated in present-day Lebanon, also had trade connections with the Somali coast. They were known for their seafaring prowess and established trade routes that extended from the Mediterranean to the Red Sea and the Indian Ocean. The Somali coast's strategic location along these trade routes made it an important hub for commerce and cultural exchange.

The ancient Greeks, through the writings of historians and geographers such as Herodotus and Strabo, also documented their knowledge of the Somali region, referring to it as 'Barbaria' or 'the land of the Berbers' (a term that was used to describe the non-Greek-speaking people of

North Africa). The Greeks were aware of the lucrative trade between the Somali coast and the Arabian Peninsula, as well as the exchange of valuable goods such as spices, incense, and precious stones.

The spread of Islām in Somalia began in the 7th century when Muslim traders and missionaries from the Arabian Peninsula ventured into the Horn of Africa. A significant testament to the early Islāmic influence in the region is the Masjid Qiblatayn, located in Zeila, in the western Awdal region of Somalia. This mosque is distinct in that it has two Qiblahs (prayer directions), which provides compelling evidence of its foundation during a pivotal period in early Islām.

The change of the Qiblah from Jerusalem to Makkah occurred around the 2nd year of the hijrah (approximately 624 AD), during the life of Prophet Muḥammad ﷺ. This alteration in the prayer direction was a watershed moment in Islāmic history. The presence of the two Qiblahs in the Masjid Qiblatayn in Somalia indicates that it was established around this transformative time, emphasising the mosque's historical significance and the rapid propagation of Islām to the Somali coast.

Moreover, legends and historical accounts suggest that some of the early companions of Prophet Muḥammad ﷺ might have sought refuge not only in the kingdoms of Ethiopia and Eritrea but also along the coastlines of

Somalia, including areas like Zeila.

Owing to its strategic position along major trade routes, the Horn of Africa played a pivotal role in commerce between the Arabian Peninsula, the Indian subcontinent, and the African continent. This geographical advantage of the Horn made the Somali coast, particularly regions like the Awdal, a magnet for Muslim traders and missionaries eager to extend both their commercial and religious reach.

As Muslim traders established trading posts and settlements along the Somali coast, they formed intricate relationships with the local population. This interaction enabled the Somali people to become acquainted with Islāmic beliefs and practices, as well as the Arabic language. Over time, many Somalis, perhaps given the background of Wāqism, found the monotheistic teachings of Islām appealing and began to adopt the religion. The process of Islāmisation in Somalia was further enhanced by the establishment of Islāmic institutions, such as mosques and madrasahs (Islāmic schools). Cities such as Zeila and Mogadishu became prominent centres of Islāmic learning, attracting scholars and theologians from across the Islāmic world.

Over the course of history, present-day Somalia saw the rise of numerous influential Muslim empires, kingdoms, and sultanates. One of the most prominent was the Kingdom of Magadazo, better known as the Sultanate of

Mogadishu. The establishment of this sultanate can be traced back to the 10th century AD, a fact illuminated by ancient Mogadishan coins from that era. Such coins not only showcase the sultanate's longevity but also highlight its early leaders, with Ismāʿīl ibn Muḥammad being one of the first recognised rulers.

For several centuries, Mogadishu stood as a beacon of prestige, serving as the primary city in 'the Land of the Berbers', the name given to the Somali coast by medieval Arab scholars. This importance was echoed by Yāqūt al-Ḥamawī, a 12th-century Syrian historian, who, during his travels, identified Mogadishu as the region's wealthiest and most influential city. He also emphasised its role as a vital Islāmic centre along the Indian Ocean.

By the 13th century AD, the city's flourishing trade relations with medieval China had earned it notable recognition, even drawing the attention of the illustrious Kublai Khān. As accounts suggest, the Mongol Emperor sent envoys to the sultanate, though their mission was fraught with challenges. The initial delegation was captured and imprisoned, leading Kublai Khān to dispatch another group to negotiate their release. Archaeological studies in the area have since unveiled an array of coins from distant lands, including China, Sri Lanka, and Vietnam. Many of these coins originated from China's Song dynasty, but there are also traces from the Ming and Qing dynasties. These discoveries underscore Mogadishu's expansive trade networks and its role as a cosmopolitan hub during its zenith.

One of the major figures of this era was Saʿīd of Mogadishu, a prominent scholar and trader who travelled extensively throughout the region. He played a pivotal role in setting up a network of Islāmic schools and centres of learning in Somalia. During his travels, Saʿīd of Mogadishu visited various parts of the Muslim world, including Egypt, Arabia, and Persia. He is known to have studied under some of the most famous Muslim scholars of the time, bringing back a wealth of knowledge and experience with him which he used to promote Islāmic education and scholarship in Somalia.

In addition to his travels throughout the Islāmic world, Saʿīd of Mogadishu also visited Bengal and China. Mogadishu was known to have studied Mandarin during his travels to China and was extensively familiar with Chinese culture and language. Saʿīd's travels to Bengal and China are a testament to the cosmopolitan nature of Somali society at that time, as well as the extent of their seafaring prowess, their interest in trade and exploration beyond their borders. His knowledge of Mandarin and insights into Chinese culture highlight the deep cultural connections and exchanges that were taking place across the Indian Ocean. These travels speak to the larger role that Somalia played in the broader Indian Ocean world, connecting East Africa to Asia.

There were also other numerous kingdoms and empires after Mogadishu, such as the Ajūrūn Sultanate (13th-17th centuries AD), the Warsangali Sultanate (13th century-present, though its peak was between the 13th and 19th centuries AD) in the northern part of Somalia, the 'Adāl Sultanate (ca. 1415 AD – 1577 AD) in the northern part of present-day Somalia and parts of Ethiopia, the Gedo Sultanate (early 18th century AD) in the southern Gedo region of Somalia, the Majirtīn Sultanate (mid-18th to late 19th century AD) in the north-eastern part of Somalia, and the Sultanate of Hūbyū (1880s-1920s).

By the 10th century AD, Islām had become the dominant religion in most Somali city-states along the coast. The influence of Islāmic culture continued to grow as more people embraced the faith, integrating Islāmic customs and traditions into their daily lives. This widespread adoption of Islām helped solidify the religion's position in Somali society and laid the groundwork for an enduring connection between the region and the rest of the Islāmic world.

One of the most significant outcomes of the Islāmisation of Somalia was the introduction of the Arabic script to the Somali language. Prior to this, Somali oral tradition was the primary means of preserving and transmitting cultural knowledge and history. The adoption of the Arabic script allowed the Somali language to be transcribed, giving rise to a written literary tradition. This development enabled the preservation and dissemination of Somali history, poetry, and other forms of literature in a more tangible and accessible format. The use of the Arabic script in Somalia also helped greater interaction with the broader Islāmic world. As a common language of scholarship and commerce throughout the Muslim world, Arabic allowed Somalis to discover its place in the larger multinational network of the medieval Muslim world.

Ibn Baṭṭūṭah, the famous Moroccan traveller and explorer who visited Somalia in the 14th century AD, wrote about his experiences in his travelogue 'Riḥlah'. He described the Somali people as being 'incredibly honest' and hospitable to strangers, noting the importance of Islām in Somali society. Ibn Baṭṭūṭah spoke highly of the hospitality and kindness of the Somali people. He remarked on how he was welcomed into the homes of strangers and treated with great respect and generosity.

He also noted the bustling nature of the port cities and the importance of trade in the region, with ships coming from as far away as China and India to exchange goods. Additionally, he documented the many mosques he visited during his travels, including the Fakhr ad-Dīn Mosque in Mogadishu, which he described as one of the most beautiful he had ever seen.

Ibn Baṭṭūṭah was particularly impressed with the level of Islāmic scholarship and learning in Somalia. He wrote about meeting many knowledgeable and pious scholars during his travels, including the famous scholar Shaykh ʿAbdiraḥmān al-Jabartī, who was known for his mastery of Islāmic law and jurisprudence. He was also struck by the emphasis on Ṣūfīsm in Somali Islām, describing his attendance of Ṣūfī gatherings and seeing the fervour and devotion of the Ṣūfī followers.

Ibn Baṭṭūṭah also supplied a detailed description of the impressive sight of the Sulṭān's parade through Mogadishu. He noted that there were four canopies of coloured silk raised over Sulṭān's head with each canopy topped by a golden bird. The Sulṭān wore a green robe made of Jerusalem fabric with loose robes from Egypt underneath. He wore silk wraps and a large turban, and musical instruments, such as drums, trumpets, and pipes were played before him.

Overall, Ibn Baṭṭūṭah's account supplies a vivid picture of life in Somalia during the 14th century AD, highlighting the wealth, culture, and diversity of the region. It serves as a valuable historical document, shedding light on a period of Somali history that is often overlooked or forgotten. It is a glimpse into the rich and vibrant Islāmic culture and society of Somalia during his time. His observations highlight the important role that Islām played in Somali society and the dedication of the Somali people to the practise and study of their faith.

In contemporary times, Somalia remains a predominantly Muslim country with an estimated 99% of the population identifying as followers of Islām. Religion continues to play a central role in the cultural, social, and political life of the country. The long history of Islām in Somalia has shaped the nation's identity and fostered a deep connection to the broader Islāmic world, which persists as an essential aspect of Somali culture today.

It is worth noting that the legacy of Sa'īd of Mogadishu and other early Somali scholars and traders has continued to the present day. The country has produced several prominent scholars and thinkers at home and in the diaspora, playing an important role in shaping the development of Islāmic thought and practise in the region and beyond. It is worth noting that even in the West, prominent young Islāmic scholars of Somali origin, such as Shaykh Yahya Raaby, Abu Taymiyyah, Ustadh Abdul Rahman Hassan, Jamal Abdinasir, AbdulAhad Dayib and my good friend Imām Mohamud Mohamed of Irshad Islamic Center in Minnesota have made significant contributions to their local communities as well as internationally and their works have inspired thousands of young people to reconnect with Islām and strengthen their faith.

The Swāḥilī Coast

The Swāḥilī Coast refers to a stretch of the East African coastline that extends from present-day Somalia in the north to Mozambique in the south. It includes the coastal regions of Kenya and Tanzania and encompasses many islands such as Zanzibar, Pemba and Mafia. The term 'Swāḥilī' itself is derived from the Arabic word 'sawāḥil', which means 'coast' or 'coastal dwellers'.

The origins of the Swāḥilī Coast can be traced back to the early interactions between the Bantu-speaking African communities and seafaring traders from the Arabian Peninsula, Persia, and South Asia. By the 8th century AD, these traders had begun to establish settlements along the East African coast, attracted by the existing maritime trade network that connected the African continent with the Indian Ocean world. As a result of these actions, the Swāḥilī people developed a unique culture that blended African, Arab, and Persian elements. They also adopted the Islāmic religion, which became an essential aspect of their identity.

The spread of Islām along the Swāḥilī Coast was a gradual process that took place over several centuries. As Arab, Persian, and other Muslim traders settled in the region, they married local women, which led to the formation of a Muslim community that was both culturally and religiously distinct from the surrounding non-Muslim populations. The adoption of Islām by the Swāḥilī people provided them with a common religious and cultural identity, allowing them to form alliances and trade with other Muslim communities in the Indian Ocean region.

The Swāḥilī city-states, such as Kilwah, Mombasa, Malindi, and Lamu, became important centres of Islāmic culture, education, and architecture. These city-states flourished through their participation in the maritime trade of goods such as gold, ivory, spices, and textiles between Africa, the Arabian Peninsula, India, and Southeast Asia. Their prosperity attracted scholars, theologians, and artisans from various parts of the Islāmic world.

Islām was an integral part of Swāḥilī daily life. Mosques were built as places of worship and learning, and madrasahs (Islāmic schools) were proved to teach the tenets of faith, the Arabic language, and other subjects. Many Swāḥilī city-states adopted the Islāmic legal system and governance structures. The Arabic script was used to transcribe the Swāḥilī language, giving rise to a written literary tradition that included religious texts, poetry, and historical chronicles.

The Islāmisation of the Swāḥilī Coast also had an impact on the region's architecture. Swāḥilī buildings incorporated elements of Islāmic design, such as the use of geometric patterns and the construction of ornate mosques, often featuring minarets and domes. Some of the most famous examples of Swāḥilī-Islāmic architecture can be found in the Great Mosque of Kilwa, the Malindī Mosque, and the Lamu Fort.

Islām began to spread in the coastal regions of Kenya around the 8th century AD. The coastal city-states of Mombasa, Malindi, and Lamu appeared as significant centres of trade, with their prosperity directly linked to their participation in the Indian Ocean trade network. As a result of this economic growth, these city-states also became centres of Islāmic soft power. Mosques and madrasahs were built, supplying spaces for worship and learning for the growing Muslim community.

Despite the growth of Islām along the coast, the spread of Islām in the interior regions of Kenya was a slower and more gradual process. Many communities in these areas kept their traditional African beliefs and practices, which persisted alongside the spread of Islām. It was not until the arrival of the Omani Arabs in the 19th century and the construction of the Uganda Railway by the British colonial government in the late 19th and early 20th centuries that Islām began to penetrate deeper into Kenya's interior.

In the contemporary period, Islām continues to be an influential presence in Kenya, particularly along the Swāḥilī Coast. The country's religious landscape is still diverse, with many communities in the interior still adhering to their traditional African beliefs and practices or adopting Christianity, which was introduced during the colonial period.

In Tanzania, the spread of Islām began around the 8th century AD, coinciding with the arrival of Arab traders and settlers on the Swāḥilī Coast. These traders were attracted by the abundant trade opportunities and set up a network of coastal city-states, such as Kilwa and Bagamoyo, which played a central role in the Indian Ocean trade. As these coastal city-states prospered through trade, they also appeared as important Islāmic centres.

Despite the growth of Islām along the coast, many communities within inland Tanzania kept their traditional African beliefs and practices. The spread of Islām into the interior of the country did occur through caravan routes, but it was a slow and gradual process. It was not until the 19th century, during the era of the Omani Arab rule in Zanzibar and the wider East African coast, that Islāmic expansion into continental Tanzania began to significantly materialise. However, even with this increased influence, many tribes adhered to traditional beliefs and practices.

Today, Tanzania is home to a vibrant Muslim community, with mosques and Islāmic schools found throughout the country. In contemporary Tanzania, Islām and Christianity have grown to become the dominant religions, whilst a minority continue to follow traditional African beliefs.

Zanzibar, a semiautonomous archipelago off the coast

of Tanzania, was conquered by Omani Arabs, who set up it as their capital. Under Omani rule, Islām became the official faith of Zanzibar. The island's economy received help from the presence of Omanis. Zanzibar became an important centre of Indian Ocean trade, with cloves, ivory, and slaves being the primary exports. The wealth generated by this trade enabled the Omani sultans to invest in the development of Zanzibar, including the construction of buildings and infrastructure, as well as the entrenchment of Islāmic practice.

The influence of Oman on Zanzibar was particularly strong during the reign of Sulṭān Saʿīd ibn Sulṭān, who ruled from 1806 AD to 1856 AD. Sulṭān Saʿīd transformed Zanzibar into a prosperous centre of trade and Afro-Arab culture. He encouraged the settlement of Arab traders and artisans on the island and established links with other Islāmic countries, such as Persia and India. The influence of Oman on Zanzibar's culture and society is still clear today, with the island's architecture, music, and arts reflecting the fusion of African and Arab cultures. Most of the population on the island is Muslim, with mosques and Islāmic schools being found throughout the archipelago.

Unfortunately, it must be noted that Zanzibar also played a significant role in the East African slave trade, which was driven by labour demands across the Middle East, India, and the Americas. Zanzibar's strategic location on the Indian Ocean made it a key centre for the slave trade. Arab traders and African intermediaries captured people from various parts of East and Central Africa and transported them to Zanzibar, where they were sold in slave markets. The slaves were then transported by dhow ships to other parts of the world.

The slave trade had a significant impact on the populations of East and Central Africa. Historians estimate that between 10 and 20 million Africans were forcibly removed from their homes and sold into slavery between the 16th and 19th centuries. In Zanzibar, the slave trade contributed to a decline in the population of the island, as well as the wider region.

The abolition of the slave trade in the 19th century marked a turning point for Zanzibar. The trade was eventually abolished in 1873, following pressure from the British government. The end of the slave trade had a significant impact on the economy of Zanzibar, as the trade had been a significant source of wealth for the island. However, the abolition of the trade also led to the development of new industries, including plantations and trade in other commodities.

Today, the legacy of the slave trade can still be felt in Zanzibar. Many of the buildings and structures associated with the slave trade, such as slave quarters and markets, still exist on the island. The slave trade is also remembered in museums and memorials, serving as solemn monuments of the devastating impact of the trade on the people and cultures of East and Central Africa.

It is important to note, however, that while slavery did exist in East Africa and Arabia, the so-called Arab slave trade is often unfairly used to attack Islām and the Arab world. The reality is that the slave trade in East Africa was not limited to Arab traders and was a continuation of the Portuguese slave trade in the region. The Portuguese were the first to set up a major slave trade in East Africa in the 15th century AD. They captured and transported people from various parts of Africa, including East and Central Africa, to Europe and the Americas. The Portuguese also introduced guns and other weapons to the region which enabled African intermediaries to capture and sell people to European and Arab traders.

Moreover, while slavery did indeed exist in Muslim and non-Muslim societies in East Africa and Arabia, it was not as pervasive or brutal as the transatlantic slave trade started by the Portuguese. In Islāmic societies, slaves had certain rights under Islāmic law, including the right to marry and the right to own property. In addition, there were religious and legal restrictions on the enslavement of Muslims.

While the slave trade in East Africa is a dark chapter in human history, it is important to understand that the trade was started and perpetuated by a variety of actors, including the Portuguese, African intermediaries, and Arab traders. It is worth noting that the Arab and Islāmic slave trades are often associated with a particular race, ethnicity or faith. The transatlantic slave trade is almost never referred to as the 'European' or 'Christian' slave trade.

The biased approach towards the Arab and Islāmic slave trade serves to absolve white Christian Europe of its historical crimes while unfairly painting Arabs, Islām, and Muslims as the sole perpetrators of slavery. It is essential that we acknowledge the historical crimes committed by all groups involved in the slave trade and avoid perpetuating manipulative narratives that look to whitewash the crimes of European nations and vilify non-Western and Islāmic cultures.

By not acknowledging the role of Europeans in the Arab slave trade and portraying it as a uniquely Islāmic and Arab phenomenon, Western institutions and a lot of the neo-orientalist Afrocentric movements that are influenced by this narrative perpetuate harmful stereotypes and contribute to a skewed understanding of history. It is time that we confront the uncomfortable truths of our shared past and work towards a more correct and inclusive portrayal of the historical events that shaped our world.

Inland East Africa

Inland East African nations, such as Mozambique,

Uganda, Rwanda, and Burundi, were introduced to Islām mainly through Arab and Swāḥilī traders who migrated into the region during the 19th century AD. While Islām did not have the same level of historical presence and cultural influence in these nations as it did in the coastal regions, its adoption by certain groups helped the establishment of Muslim communities and the spread of Islāmic practices.

Islāmic culture also flourished in Mozambique with the construction of mosques, madrasahs, and other Islāmic institutions. These centres of learning eased the spread of Islāmic knowledge and helped to set up a thriving Muslim community in the region. However, the adoption of Islām in the interior regions of Mozambique was a more gradual process, with many communities continuing to follow their traditional African beliefs and practices. Over time, Islāmic influence expanded beyond the coastal regions and Islām became an integral part of Mozambique's cultural and religious landscape.

Today, Islām is a significant religion in Mozambique with approximately 18% of the population identifying as Muslim. The country's Islāmic heritage is reflected in its architecture, literature, and cuisine, which incorporate both African and Arab influences. The spread of Islām in Mozambique is a testament to the power of cultural exchange and the enduring legacy of trade and commerce in shaping the region's religious and cultural identity.

In Uganda, during the late 19th and early 20th centuries, Islām began to gain greater acceptance amongst certain groups in the northern region. In Rwanda and Burundi, however, Islām's adoption was largely limited to certain ethnic groups, such as the Tutsi and Swāḥilī. It did not have a significant impact on the broader population.

It is also essential to highlight that the Bāʿalawī scholars played a significant role in spreading Islām in East Africa, particularly in Tanzania, Kenya, and Uganda. The Bāʿalawī family is one of the most influential and respected Islāmic families in the world. Descended from the Prophet Muḥammad ﷺ, the Bāʿalawī family originates from Ḥaḍramawt, a region in Yemen, and has a significant presence in its main city, Tarīm. Among these notable Bāʿalawī scholars is Ḥabīb Ṣāliḥ ibn ʿAlawī Jamal al-Layl, who was born in the Ḥaḍramawt but settled in Lamu, a small town on Lamu Island, which in turn is a part of the Lamu Archipelago in Kenya in the early 20th century.

Ḥabīb Ṣāliḥ was well-versed in Islāmic traditional medicine and herbalism and is perhaps best known for his role in initiating the annual Mawlid Festival in Lamu, celebrating the birth of the Prophet Muḥammad ﷺ. The festival became an important cultural event in Lamu and attracted visitors from various countries. During the Mawlid, the streets of Lamu are decorated with colourful lights and banners, and the air is filled with the sounds of drums, songs, and religious chants. The event involves a week-long series of processions, recitations, and other religious rituals, with participants from across East Africa and beyond. The festivities culminate in a grand procession, where participants parade through the town carrying banners and flags and reciting praise to the Prophet ﷺ. This event has special significance in Lamu, where it has been celebrated for over 100 years.

Ḥabīb Ṣāliḥ was highly respected and influential among the local community in Lamu, beloved for his emphasis on a deep-rooted, spiritual connection with God and Prophet Muḥammad ﷺ. He passed away in 1935, but his legacy continues among a new generation of Bāʿalawī and East African scholars. Today, Bāʿalawī scholars continue to have a significant impact on the Islāmic community in East Africa and beyond, with their teachings and practices continuing to inspire many Muslims worldwide. Their emphasis on spirituality has resonated with many, and their efforts to promote unity and cooperation among different Muslim communities have helped to strengthen faith in the region.

The East African Islands

Zanzibar is not the only East African island with a Muslim presence. In fact, many of the islands in the region have a rich Islāmic heritage. The spread of Islām on the Comoros began in the 8th century AD with the arrival of

Arab traders and settlers. These traders and settlers were primarily from Oman and the Arabian Peninsula, and they showed trading posts on the islands of Comoros given its location along the East African coast. The Comorians embraced Islām over time. Today, nearly 99% of the population of the Comoros identifies as Muslim, making it one of the most Muslim-majority countries in the world.

Islām was introduced to Madagascar in the 10th century AD by Arab traders and missionaries who sailed across the Indian Ocean from the Arabian Peninsula and the East African coast. Religion gradually spread to various parts of the island and coexisted with traditional Malagasy beliefs and customs, although its progress was not always straightforward. While some communities readily embraced Islām and converted to the faith, others were resistant and blended it with their traditional beliefs. Today, approximately 7% of the population of Madagascar is Muslim, with the majority living in the northern and western parts of the country.

Islām arrived in Mauritius in the 18th century through the arrival of Muslim slaves from East Africa. This small community were then joined by the muslims who were part of the large numbers of indentured labourers from India - who were brought to the island to work on sugarcane plantations during the colonial era after the abolition of slavery - in the 19th century. Over time, these Muslims settled in Mauritius and formed communities, building mosques and practising their religion.

In Mauritius, the Muslim community initially faced discrimination and marginalisation from the colonial authorities and the dominant Christian community. However, over time, they were able to set up themselves and gain recognition as an important religious and cultural minority in the country.

Ṣūfī orders also played an important role in the spread of Islām in Mauritius, particularly in the 19th and early 20th centuries. These orders, which emphasised spiritual experience and personal devotion, attracted many people to the faith and helped to prove a strong Muslim identity on the island. Today, Islām is one of the major religions in Mauritius, with approximately 17% of the population identifying as Muslim. The Muslim community in Mauritius is diverse, consisting of people of Indian, Arab and African descent, whilst being characterised by a blend of Sunnī and Ṣūfī traditions.

The Horn of Africa

It is well known that Islām has been present in the Horn of Africa since the very beginning of the religion, as we discussed in the previous chapter. Over time, Islām continued to spread in the Horn of Africa through a combination of peaceful means, including trade and missionary activities, as well as through political and military conquests. The spread of Islām in the region was influenced by various factors, including the location of important trade routes, the presence of significant Muslim communities in nearby regions, and the conversion of local rulers and elites.

Islām arrived in Ethiopia, Eritrea, and Djibouti in the early days of the religion, brought by Arab traders and missionaries who travelled across the Red Sea from the Arabian Peninsula. In the years following the death of Najāshī, the early Muslim community in Ethiopia faced persecution from Christian rulers who saw them as a threat to the Christian faith. As a result, the Muslim community was forced to practise their religion in secret, and faced significant obstacles in spreading their faith throughout the region.

It was not until the 16th century AD that Islām was able to set up a significant presence in Ethiopia. This was due in large part to the conversion of the Muslim warlord Aḥmad ibn Ibrāhīm al-Ghāzī, also known as Ahmed Gragn, who launched a series of military campaigns against the Christian rulers of Ethiopia. Ahmed Gragn was able to defeat the Ethiopian forces and establish a Muslim sultanate in the eastern part of the country, centred on the city of Harar.

Harar became an important centre of Islāmic power. The city was ruled by a series of Muslim sultanates, all of whom contributed to its role as a nexus of Islāmic civilisation. Despite the active emphasis on religious policy, the sultanates were still known for their tolerance of different religions and cultures while actively encouraging the growth of the Muslim community in the city.

One of the most significant features of Harar is its old town, surrounded by a wall built in the 16th century AD. The old town holds many mosques and other Islāmic sites, including the Jāmiʿ Mosque, which is the oldest mosque in the city and dates to the 10th century AD. It is also home to several traditional houses and other buildings, many of which were built in the 19th century and reflect the unique architectural style of the region.

Harar's cosmopolitan character - which saw significant populations of Muslims, Christians, and Jews living side by side - and its tolerance and inclusiveness helped foster a climate of religious and cultural pluralism, which contributed to the growth and spread of Islām. Today, Harar remains an important centre of Ethiopian Islām and continues to attract visitors from around the world.

Eritrea also has a long history of Muslim presence, dating back to the early days of Islām. The religion first arrived in the region through Arab traders who travelled across the Red Sea from the Arabian Peninsula. Over time, the Muslim community grew and proved strong roots in the region, particularly in the coastal city of Massawa.

The spread of Islām in Eritrea was largely driven by trade and commerce and benefited from the influence of neighbouring Muslim societies in the Red Sea region. Today, a large portion of the population of Eritrea is Muslim.

It is also worth noting that some scholars and historians have disputed the location of the Kingdom of Axum, which is traditionally believed to have been in Ethiopia. Some argue that the kingdom may have been in what is now Eritrea, and that the ruler known as Najāshī may have been based in the city of Adulis, an important capital of the Red Sea region. While this theory is still a subject of debate, it underscores the complex history of Eritrea and the importance of continued scholarship and research into its past.

In Djibouti, Islām arrived in the 9th century AD, brought by Arab traders who travelled across the Red Sea from the Arabian Peninsula and quickly became the dominant faith following multiple mass conversions. Djibouti's strategic location at the entrance to the Red Sea guaranteed its importance as an axis of the Muslim world. The city became an important stopover point for Muslim traders travelling between the Arabian Peninsula, Africa, and beyond. This trade helped foster a cosmopolitan character in the city, with significant populations of Muslims from various parts of the world living and working side by side. Today, nearly all of the population of Djibouti is Muslim, with the majority following the Sunnī branch of Islām.

The history of Islām in East Africa is a rich and complex one that deserves to be explored and studied. From the early days of the Islāmic empires to the present day, the spread of Islām in the region has been shaped by a variety of factors, including trade, migration, and the influence of neighbouring societies. In this chapter, we have examined the history of the spread of Islām in East Africa, and in the following chapters, we will explore how the people of these countries affected the wider Muslim world, including the Middle East and Asia. Through this exploration, we hope to gain a deeper understanding of the ways in which Islām has shaped and been shaped by the diverse cultures and societies of East Africa.

It is important to note that the history of Islām in East Africa is vast and complex, and it is impossible to do justice to it in just one chapter. We have only scratched the surface, and there is much more to explore and learn. It is crucial that we continue to elevate and amplify the voices of East African scholars and intellectuals who can offer a more nuanced and detailed understanding of their history and legacy. Only by doing so can we begin to fully appreciate the significance of East Africa's contributions to the wider Muslim world, including the Middle East and Asia.

Chapter 4:
SUDAN & THE ZANJ

On the journey through the annals of classical Arabic and Islāmic history, there are certain terms which carry profound meaning and shape our understanding of regions and peoples. Among these, 'Sudan' and 'Zanj' stand out, serving as all-encompassing terms that illuminate the rich tapestry of cultures, languages, and peoples. In classical Arabic, the term 'Sūdān' refers to the region south of Egypt, stretching from the Nile River to the central and western parts of Africa. Its etymology stems from the Arabic word 'as-Sūd' or 'sūd', meaning 'black' or 'dark'.

In today's world, when we mention Sudan, it typically refers to a specific nation-state. During the Islāmic era, however, the term 'Sūdān' held broader significance as it encompassed not only the lands that now include present-day Sudan and South Sudan, but also extended to the wider geographic region and its diverse people. In this historical context, the term 'Sūdān' served as a descriptor for black communities and included the entirety of Sub-Saharan Africa. Even under the shadow of colonialism, the term 'Sūdān' persisted and was used to describe West Africa. In that context used by the colonial powers, West Africa was known as 'Western Sudan'.

In classical Arabic and Islāmic terminology, 'Zanj' appeared as a term to refer to the East African region, particularly the coastal areas of present-day Somalia, Kenya, Tanzania, and Mozambique. Its origins can be traced back to the Persian word 'Zang', meaning 'black' or 'Negro'. The Zanj region was renowned for its valuable commodities, including ivory and gold. However, it was also a region marked by the brutal trade of enslaved Africans. As a result, the term 'Zanj' became associated with these enslaved individuals who were brought from the East African coast and sold across various parts of the Islāmic world, including the Arabian Peninsula and Iraq.

When examining the history of Sudan and Zanj, it is crucial to recognise the profound impact that Africans from these regions had on the Arab and Muslim worlds throughout the Islāmic period. Evidence of this impact can be found in the works of renowned scholars. As early as the 8th century AD, the polymath, al-Jāhiẓ, wrote the famous (or infamous) 'Fakhr as-Sūdān 'alā al-Biḍān' (The Glory of the Black Race over the White Race)'. This was followed by Ibn Jawzī's 'Tanwīr al-Ghabash fī Faḍli is-Sūdān wa al-

Ḥabash' (The Illuminating Twilight Concerning the Virtue of the Sudanese and Abyssinians) in the 11th century AD and Imām Suyūṭī's 'Raf'u Shȧni il-Ḥabshān' (Elevating the Prestige of Abyssinians) in the 14th century AD. These works focused on the virtues and contributions of Sudanese and Abyssinian peoples.

The Zanj Rebellion

Historically, the Zanj name became synonymous with rebellion and resistance. In the 9th century AD, a significant revolt known as the Zanj Rebellion erupted in southern Iraq, led by enslaved Africans who rebelled against their oppressive conditions. This rebellion challenged the prevailing power structures of the time and left an indelible mark on the collective memory of the region.

After the time of the Rāshidūn Caliphate, the Umayyad Caliphate rose to power, governing a vast empire that stretched from Spain to Persia. This rapid expansion also promoted the sale of African slaves, who were increasingly brought into the region because of campaigns and thriving trade routes. During the rise of the Umayyad Caliphate, African slaves were sourced from various regions through a combination of military conquests, trade networks, and indigenous African kingdoms involved in the trans-Saharan slave trade. The Abbasid Caliphate, which succeeded the Umayyads, inherited the complex social and economic landscape marked by the presence of those African slaves.

One significant source of African slaves was West Africa, particularly the regions of present-day Mali, Niger, Senegal, and Mauritania. The Arab conquerors of the Umayyad and Abbasid Caliphates engaged in military campaigns that brought them into contact with local African societies. In the process, many individuals were captured as prisoners of war and enslaved.

Another major source of African slaves was the East African coast, including regions such as modern-day Somalia, Kenya, Tanzania, and Mozambique. These coastal areas were key nodes in the Indian Ocean trade network, where Arab and Persian traders established commercial ties with African merchants. Slavery, unfortunately, became a by-product of these trade interactions. Indigenous African kingdoms and rulers also played a role in easing the enslavement of their own people, capturing and selling individuals from rival communities or even their own subjects to Arab slave traders.

Individuals were enslaved through various methods. Some were captured during raids in villages and towns, while others were taken as captives during battles or wars. Many were forcibly transported from their homelands and subjected to gruelling journeys across the Sahara or the Indian Ocean. These enslaved Africans endured horrific conditions, including physical abuse, separation from their families, and the loss of their freedom and cultural heritage. Once in the Arab and Muslim world, African slaves were primarily employed as domestic servants, agricultural labourers, or in various skilled and unskilled occupations. They formed a significant part of the workforce that contributed to the economic prosperity of the Umayyad and Abbasid Caliphates.

The enslavement of Africans during this period was deeply rooted in a complex web of economic, social, and political dynamics. It was fuelled by the demand for labour, the desire for wealth, and the prevailing ideologies of racial superiority that perpetuated the subjugation of the black individual. As Professor Johnathan Brown pointed out in his book 'Blackness & Islam', by this time, Islāmic civilisation inherited stereotypes about Black Africans from the Greco-Roman conviction that shaped both body and personality and from Judeo-Christian lore about Africans being 'cursed' with blackness and enslavement. Though prominent Muslim scholars opposed these ideas as antithetical to the Qur'ān, the bulk of Islāmic tradition indulged and added to this body of material, which justified and perpetuated the subjugation and exploitation of Black Africans in Islāmic societies.

While it is important to acknowledge the historical reality of African enslavement, it is equally crucial to recognise the resistance and resilience displayed by enslaved Africans throughout history. The Zanj Rebellion stands as a poignant testament to their defiance and their quest for freedom and justice. Under the Umayyad and Abbasid

Caliphates, the Zanj were subjected to backbreaking labour on plantations, in salt marshes, and in the construction of cities and infrastructure. They endured harsh working conditions, minimal provisions, and relentless physical and psychological abuse. As the Abbasid Caliphate emerged its rule, the exploitation of African slaves intensified. The ruling elite thrived on the subjugation and commodification of human beings stripped of their dignity and agency.

This deplorable treatment, coupled with the growing awareness of their collective strength, fuelled the spirit of resistance among the Zanj. The oppressive conditions they endured became the catalyst for their rebellion. The Zanj rebels, driven by a shared desire for freedom and justice, looked to challenge the power structures that had perpetuated their suffering. The fall of the Umayyad Caliphate and the next rise of the Abbasids created a climate of political and social unrest, which supplied an opportunity for the Zanj Rebellion to take hold. As the Abbasid forces struggled to combine their authority and faced internal divisions, the Zanj rebels capitalised on these vulnerabilities, successfully asserting their autonomy in key regions.

The rebellion erupted in 869 AD and lasted until 883 AD. It unfolded in the vicinity of Baṣrah, a city in present-day southern Iraq, and was spearheaded by a remarkable individual named ʿAlī ibn Muḥammad, who appeared as a charismatic and influential leader, rallying thousands of

Zanj and other enslaved individuals in a collective struggle against the oppressive Abbasid Caliphate. The rebellion attracted a diverse range of participants, including South-eastern Africans and Arabs, reflecting a shared desire for liberation from the bonds of slavery.

ʿAlī ibn Muḥammad, the leader of the Zanj Rebellion, is still an enigmatic figure with conflicting accounts about his background and lineage. According to one version, his paternal grandfather traced his ancestry to the ʿAbdul Qays tribe, while his mother belonged to the Banū Asad ibn Khuzaymah. These affiliations suggest an Arab heritage, although some later commentators have guessed about a possible Persian origin. However, many historians dismiss that notion. It is also worth noting that ʿAlī himself claimed to be a descendant of ʿAlī ibn Abī Ṭālib, who was the son-in-law of the Prophet Muḥammad ﷺ and the fourth caliph of the Rāshidūn Caliphate. This claim, however, was widely rejected by Muslim historians of the era.

The ambiguity surrounding ʿAlī ibn Muḥammad's background reflects the complexity of the historical record and the challenges of tracing individual lineages accurately, particularly in periods marked by social upheaval and political unrest. The focus of the Zanj Rebellion was not on ʿAlī's personal lineage but on the collective grievances and aspirations of the oppressed and marginalised individuals involved.

While ʿAlī's specific heritage is still a subject of debate, his leadership and ability to mobilise a diverse range of people, including Zanj, Arabs, and other groups, are noteworthy. Regardless of his background, ʿAlī played a crucial role in uniting and inspiring thousands of rebels, leading them into a protracted struggle against the Abbasid Caliphate.

Commencing in September 869 AD, the Zanj Rebellion initially focused on the regions of Iraq and al-Aḥwāz (modern Khuzestan Province) within the Abbasid Caliphate. The Zanj rebels, despite facing superior arms, employed guerrilla warfare tactics and highlighted their adaptability in raiding towns, villages, and enemy camps. They were skilled at seising weapons, horses, food, and captives while freeing fellow slaves. To deter retaliation, they burned captured areas to delay the enemy's pursuit.

The rebellion gained strength over time, with the rebels constructing fortresses, developing a naval fleet to navigate the region's canals and rivers, collecting taxes in territories under their control and even minting their own coins. Despite efforts by the Abbasid government to suppress the revolt, including a retaliatory campaign in 872 AD, the Zanj remained resilient and continued to pose a significant challenge to the Caliph.

The inability of the Abbasid forces to decisively crush the rebellion was due, in part, to the Anarchy at Sāmarrā, a period of internal disorder and conflict within the Abbasid Caliphate. The central government in Abbasid Sāmarrā was paralyzed, allowing various provinces to fall into the hands of rebels and leading to a decrease in taxation revenues. This weakened the government's ability to effectively respond to the Zanj uprising. Additionally, 'Alī ibn Muḥammad used his connections with influential slaves in the capital and travelled to different regions, including Bahrain, to rally support for his cause. His tactics included adopting slogans from the egalitarian doctrine of the Khārijites, inscribing banners and coins with Khārijite expressions, and proclaiming himself the 'Chief of the Zanjites'.

The rebellion spread beyond Baṣrah as the Zanj rebels expanded their activities to the north, occupying marshlands, sacking towns, and advancing towards Baghdad, the then capital of the Abbasid caliphate. The Abbasid government regained the initiative in the war in late 879 AD, and after a prolonged siege, the rebel stronghold of Al-Mukhtārah fell in August 883 AD. The rebellion was ultimately quelled, with 'Alī ibn Muḥammad and most of the rebel commanders either killed or captured.

Both the rebels and their opponents engaged in looting and massacres, worsening the death toll and humanitarian crisis. Estimating the number of casualties in the conflict is challenging, as historical accounts supply widely variable figures. Contemporary writers, such as Al-Masʿūdī and As-Ṣūlī, offered numbers ranging from 500,000 to 2,500,000 casualties. The rebellion left a trail of devastation, including burned cities, disrupted trade, and severe shortages of essential resources such as food and water.

The Zanj Rebellion stands for a complex chapter in history, with varying interpretations about the composition of the rebels and the long-term effects of the uprising. Scholars, such as Ghadā Hāshem Talḥamī, argue against equating the Zanj solely with East Africans, pointing out that the rebellion was not exclusively led by slaves but also involved individuals from different social backgrounds, including free Arabs and various groups from the Baṣrah region. Talḥamī emphasises that contemporary sources do not explicitly link the term 'Zanj' solely to the East African coast or show a specific origin for the rebels. Instead, the rebellion was a social and religious uprising that stood for the grievances of the oppressed and marginalised within Baṣrah.

Another historian, M.A. Shaban, challenges the belief that the Zanj Rebellion was primarily a slave revolt. Shaban argues that while some runaway slaves took part, most of the rebels were Arabs and free East Africans. He suggests that if the revolt had been led exclusively by slaves, they would not have possessed the necessary resources to sustain the rebellion for such an extended period.

While the rebellion ultimately met its end with the fall of Al-Mukhtārah and the defeat of its leaders, it left an indelible mark on the collective memory of the region. The Zanj Rebellion serves as a testament to the resilience, agency, and collective action of those who looked to challenge the oppressive system. It stays an important chapter in the history of social uprisings and resistance, shedding light on the struggles faced by marginalised communities. The Zanj Rebellion not only aimed to secure freedom for the enslaved Africans but also looked to challenge the very foundations of the Abbasid Caliphate.

Black History in the Islāmic World

Beyond war efforts, just as in the pre-Islāmic Jāhilī period and during the time of the Prophet Muḥammad ﷺ, many Africans or 'sūdān' made significant contributions to Arab and Muslim societies during the Middle Ages. Their intellectual prowess, revolutionary spirit, and deep devotion to Islām left a permanent mark on the Islāmic empires of the time.

Among these remarkable individuals were the first Muftīs of Makkah, Egypt and Syria, who hailed from Bilād as-Sūdān and the Zanj. These scholars played a pivotal role in shaping the religious and legal discourse of their respective regions and supplying guidance and ability on matters of Islāmic jurisprudence. Their authority and knowledge were highly regarded, and they were instrumental in proving the foundations of Islāmic scholarship in these crucial centres of the Muslim world.

Furthermore, Sudan and Zanj were home to key narrators of ḥadīth, the narrations of sayings and actions of the Prophet Muḥammad ﷺ. These narrators meticulously preserved and transmitted the Prophetic traditions, ensuring their authenticity and widespread dissemination. Their dedication to the preservation of Islāmic knowledge greatly influenced the development of Islāmic thought and scholarship.

In addition to religious scholars, Sudan and Zanj produced brilliant black intellectuals who excelled in various fields of study. These intellectuals contributed to diverse disciplines, including philosophy, mathematics, astronomy, medicine, and literature. Their ground-breaking ideas and advancements enriched the intellectual landscape of the Islāmic empires, fostering a culture of innovation and intellectual exchange. We will discuss some of these enigmatic figures here in this chapter.

In addition to individuals from Sudan and Zanj, it is important to acknowledge the presence of black Arab people who would be racialised as black in the modern world due to their skin complexion and phenotype, regardless of their ancestral origins. These black Arab intellectuals, scholars, and leaders played a vital role in shaping various aspects of Arab and Muslim history. Their achievements spanned different fields, including literature, poetry, science, governance, and military leadership. They were influential figures whose impact resonated across the Arab world.

Scholars

Saʿīd ibn Jubayr

Saʿīd ibn Jubayr (died 714 AD) was a prominent figure among the Tābiʿīn, the generation of Muslims who succeeded the companions of the Prophet Muḥammad ﷺ. He was born in Kufa, Iraq, and belonged to the Asad tribe. Saʿīd ibn Jubayr was known for his knowledge, piety, and dedication to seeking religious knowledge and understanding.

Ibn Kathīr, in his work 'Al-Bidāyah wa an-Nihāyah', references Ibn Khallikān's description of Saʿīd ibn Jubayr. According to Ibn Khallikān, Saʿīd ibn Jubayr, the son of Hishām al-Asadī, belonged to the Banū Wālibah tribe and was a mawlā (a client or freedman) from Kufa. Ibn Khallikān further notes that Saʿīd ibn Jubayr had a dark black complexion. He was a student of several renowned companions of the Prophet Muḥammad ﷺ, including Ibn ʿAbbās, ʿAbdullāh ibn ʿUmar, and ʿAbdullāh ibn ʿAmr ibn Al-ʿĀs. Saʿīd ibn Jubayr was highly respected for his intelligence, virtue, and correct memorization of ḥadīths.

He was known for his eloquence and his ability to interpret and explain the Qur'ān. He was a proficient scholar in the fields of fiqh (Islāmic jurisprudence), tafsīr (Qur'ānic exegesis), and ḥadīth. He travelled extensively, seeking knowledge from various scholars in different regions, including Ḥijāz, Egypt, and Yemen.

His views and opinions on religious matters were highly regarded and sought after by scholars of his time. Sa'īd ibn Jubayr was known for his adherence to the principles of the Qur'ān and Sunnah and his strong stance against injustice and oppression.

He was a steadfast critic of the Umayyad Caliphate and openly expressed his disapproval of its policies and practices. Unfortunately, Sa'īd ibn Jubayr's life was cut short when he was assassinated during the reign of the Umayyad governor, Al-Ḥajjāj ibn Yūsuf. The details surrounding his assassination vary in different accounts, but it is believed that he was killed in the month of Sha'bān in the year 714 AD.

'Aṭā ibn Abī Rabāḥ

'Aṭā ibn Abī Rabāḥ was a renowned early Muslim scholar and ḥadīth transmitter who held the position of 'the Muftī of Makkah' during the late seventh and early eighth centuries AD. He was born in the town of Muwallad il-Janad in Yemen. While the exact year of his birth is debated, it is generally accepted that he was born during the reign of ʿUthmān ibn ʿAffan, approximately 25 AH/646 AD. His mother was a Nubian basket weaver, and his father, Aslam, was described as having a dark complexion and a flat nose. ʿAṭā himself had physical disabilities, including a limp and blindness later in life.

Raised in Makkah as a mawlā (client) of Abū Khuthaym al-Fihrī, a member of the Qurayshī tribe, ʿAṭā initially worked as a Qurʾān teacher before gaining recognition for his ability in fiqh (jurisprudence). He was later appointed as the Muftī of Makkah by the Umayyad rulers and taught in the Masjid al-Ḥarām, where he also lived. During his time in Makkah, ʿAṭā had the opportunity to meet and narrate ḥadīth from notable companions of Prophet Muḥammad ﷺ, such as Ibn ʿAbbās, Abū Hurayrah, and Jābir ibn ʿAbdillāh. Among his distinguished students were Ibn Jurayj and Qays ibn Saʿd.

ʿAṭā was known for his piety and virtuous character. He led a simple life, performed the Ḥajj pilgrimage approximately seventy times, and could recite 200 verses from Sūrah al-Baqarah in ṣalāh (prayer) without moving, even in old age. His scholarship extended to various areas, including fiqh and *ḥadīth*. People sought his knowledge and ḥadīth narrations, and he transmitted knowledge to many narrators of ḥadīth among the Tābiʿīn and those who came after them. Some of the prominent scholars who learned from him include; Mālik ibn Dīnār, Az-Zuhrī, Al-Aʿmash, Qatādah, Mujāhid, Ayyūb As-Sakhtiyānī, Manṣūr ibn Al-Muʿtamir, Yaḥyā ibn Abī Kathīr, Abu Ḥanīfah, and others.

During the Umayyad period, it was proclaimed during the days of Hajj that no one should issue a fatwā (legal edict) except ʿAṭā ibn Abī Rabāḥ. Abū Ḥanīfah spoke highly of him, and others praised his moral character, virtue, knowledge, piety, and dedication to worship. He was respected as a muftī and was known for centering his speeches on the remembrance of Allāh. When asked a question, he supplied the best answer.

An incident narrated by Al-Aṣmaʿī illustrates the respect and reverence people had for ʿAṭa. When he visited ʿAbdul Malik ibn Marwān, the Caliph, in Makkah, ʿAbdul Malik stood up to greet him and invited him to sit beside him on the bed. ʿAṭa recommended that ʿAbdul Malik fear Allāh and fulfil his responsibilities towards the construction and maintenance of the Ḥaram, the descendants of the Muhājirīn and Anṣār, and the people in the frontier regions who were the defenders of Muslims. ʿAbdul Malik acknowledged his advice and pledged to act accordingly. ʿAṭā's focus on the concerns of others and his lack of personal demands impressed ʿAbdul Malik, who recognised it as true honour and steadfastness.

Biographical sources differ on the year of his death, but it is believed to be approximately 115 AH/733 AD.

Yazīd ibn Abī Ḥabīb

Abū Rajā' Yazīd ibn Abī Ḥabīb al-Azdi al-Maṣrī (53 AH - 128 AH/673 - 745 AD) was a renowned jurist and scholar among the trustworthy narrators of the Tābi'īn (successors to the companions of the Prophet Muḥammad ﷺ). He served as the Muftī of Egypt and was highly respected for his knowledge and ability. Born in Fusṭāṭ, Egypt, during the caliphate of Mu'āwiyah ibn Abī Sufyān, approximately 673 AD, he was of Nubian origin and had a dark complexion. His lineage can be traced back to the region of Dongola in modern-day Sudan. He received knowledge from some companions of the Prophet ﷺ and prominent Tābi'īn who lived in Egypt, including 'Abdullāh ibn al-Ḥārith, from whom he directly learned.

Yazīd ibn Abī Ḥabīb's father, Suwayd ibn Abī Ḥabīb, was a slave of Nubian descent who was brought to Egypt as a captive during the campaign led by 'Abdullāh ibn Sa'd ibn Abī is-Sarḥ against the Nubians in 13 AH. Suwayd embraced Islām in Egypt, married, and had children, including Yazīd.

Yazīd possessed extensive knowledge of jurisprudence, ḥadīth, history, warfare, and matters related to the conquest and governance of Egypt. The Caliph, 'Umar ibn 'Abdul-'Azīz, was the one who selected him alongside two others with the responsibility of issuing fatwās (legal edicts) in Egypt during his reign. He was soon after highly regarded as the Muftī of Egypt during his time and was among the pioneering scholars of fiqh. (Islāmic jurisprudence) in the region. His trustworthiness in transmitting ḥadīth was recognised by scholars, and he was mentioned by Ibn Sa'd as 'trustworthy and well-versed in ḥadīth' and is one of the narrators in Ṣaḥīḥ al-Bukhārī.

Most of what is known about him comes from the works of Al-Kindī in his book 'The Rulers of Egypt and Their Judge,', as well as Ibn 'Abdul Ḥakam in his work on the conquest of Egypt and Morocco. Abū Sa'īd ibn Yūnus said, "He was the Muftī of the people of Egypt in his time, forbearing, wise, and the first to establish knowledge in Egypt, speaking about the permissible and the prohibited, and legal matters. Previously, people would only discuss turmoil, battles, and inciting evil."

The renowned scholar, Aḥmad ibn Ḥanbal, said, "Allāh bestows the treasure of knowledge to one whom He loves. If knowledge would have been kept only for a specific people, then those with the noblest lineage would be most deserving of it. However, 'Aṭā (ibn Abī Rabāḥ) was an Abyssinian slave, Yazīd ibn Abī Ḥabīb was a Nubian, and Ḥasan al-Baṣrī and Ibn Sīrīn were both slaves."

Aside from his vast knowledge, Yazīd was also known for his love of justice, and he boldly spoke out against oppression. Once, the governor of Egypt came to visit him and enquired about his opinion about performing the prayer with the blood of a flea on one's clothes. Hearing this, Yazīd shouted, "Daily, you spill the blood of Allāh's creation, and you now come asking about the blood of a flea."

It is truly remarkable to acknowledge that the first Muftī of Egypt, its highest religious authority, was a black African man, especially as he laid the foundations for Egypt to later become the centre of learning in the Muslim world.

Ḥabīb Ibn Abī Thābit

Ḥabīb ibn Abī Thābit was a respected Imām, renowned for preserving ḥadīth and recognised as a jurist and muftī in Kufa, in modern-day Iraq. His honorific title was Abū Yaḥyā, and he belonged to the Quraysh clan of the Asad tribe. Habīb's father was named Qays ibn Dīnār, although some sources claim it was Qays ibn Hind or simply Hind. He was described as having a black complexion.

Ḥabīb was known for narrating from notable figures such as Ibn ʿUmar, Ibn ʿAbbās, and Umm Salama. However, there are claims that he might not have directly heard from them. His narrations from these figures are documented in Ibn Mājah. He also narrated from Ḥakīm ibn Ḥizām, and this narration is recorded in Al-Jāmiʿ at-Tirmidhī. In addition, Ḥabīb narrated from Anas ibn Mālik, Zaid ibn Arqam, Abī Wāʾil, and several others, proving himself as a prominent scholar of his time.

One of Ḥabīb's unique attributes was his ability to connect with scholars both older and younger than him, such as 'Aṭā ibn Abī Rabāḥ, who was one of his teachers and Ḥabīb also narrated from him. Many others, including Ḥusayn, Manṣūr, and Al-A'mash, also held him in high regard. Ultimately, Ḥabīb ibn Abī Thābit was considered a pillar in the community. There is a notable account that Abū Bakr ibn 'Iyāsh narrated from Abū Yaḥyā al-Qattāt, saying that when Ḥabīb arrived in Ṭā'if, the reception he received was as if a prophet had entered the city.

Makḥūl al-Shāmī

Makḥūl was known for his deep black skin colour, a testament to his Nubian heritage. However, it was his profound knowledge and sagacity that made him an acclaimed scholar of his era. In an epoch marked by the passing of the four "Abādilah' — illustrious companions of the Prophet ﷺ who were known for their knowledge and all shared the name 'Abdullāh — jurisprudential guidance across Islāmic realms shifted. While places such as Makkah, Yemen, Yamāmah, Baṣrah, Kufa, and Khorasan turned to the Mawālī (freed slaves and non-Arab Muslims) for scholarly leadership, Madīnah remained under the Qurayshī jurist, Sa'īd ibn Al-Musayyib. However, in Shām (modern-day Syria and surrounding regions), Makḥūl's brilliance shone the brightest.

'Abdur Raḥmān ibn Zaid ibn Aslam said, "When the "Abādilah' died ('Abdullāh ibn 'Abbās, 'Abdullāh ibn Az-Zubair, 'Abdullāh ibn 'Umar, and 'Abdullāh ibn 'Amr ibn Al-'Āṣ), the jurisprudence in all countries shifted to the Mawālī (freed slaves and non-Arab Muslims); 'Aṭā being the jurist of Makkah, Ṭāwūs of Yemen, Yaḥyā ibn Abī Kathīr of Yamāmah, Al-Ḥasan of Baṣrah, Ibrāhīm an-Nakha'ī of Kufa, Makḥūl of Shām, 'Aṭā al-Khurasānī of Khorasan, except in Madīnah where Allāh blessed it with a Qurayshī jurist, Sa'īd ibn Al-Musayyib."

Esteemed contemporaries spoke highly of him. Az-Zuhrī mentioned him among the four main scholars of that era, saying, "There are four scholars - Sa'īd ibn Al-Musayyib in Madīnah, Al-Sha'bī in Kufa, Al-Ḥasan in Baṣrah, and Makḥūl - in Shām." Further recognition came from Sulaymān ibn Mūsā, as Sa'īd ibn 'Abdul 'Azīz said that Sulaymān ibn Mūsā used to say, "When knowledge comes to us from Ḥijāz from Az-Zuhrī, we accept it. When it comes from Shām from Makḥūl, we accept it. When it comes from the island from Maymūn ibn Mihrān, we accept it. In addition, when it comes from Iraq from Al-Ḥasan, we accept it. These four are the scholars of the people during the rule of Hishām (ibn 'Abdul Malik, the tenth Umayyad Caliph)."

The fact that he was a man of Nubian origin, whose complexion was very black, neither hindered his stature nor dimmed his brilliance in the scholarly circles of Shām. Al-Dhahabī mentions the difference in opinions regarding Makḥūl's allegiance. It is believed he might have been owned by a woman from the Hudhaylī tribe; others suggest an Umayyad woman, while some say he was owned by Saʿīd ibn al-ʿĀṣ, who gifted him to a Hudhaylī woman who then freed him. However, the most authentic opinion was that he was of Nubian ancestry and was merely captured and then relocated. However, irrespective of his origins, Makḥūl's contributions to Islāmic scholarship were undeniably vast.

He travelled in pursuit of ḥadīth knowledge. He said, "I travelled the entire world seeking knowledge. I was freed in Egypt, and I did not leave any knowledge there without getting it, in my opinion. Then, I went to Iraq, then Madīnah, and did not leave any knowledge there without obtaining it, in my opinion. Then, I came to Levant and thoroughly searched it." He also said, "Whatever I commit to memory, I find it whenever I need it." He then settled in Damascus, which is why Al-Dhahabī in his 'Siyar Aʿlām al-Nubalā'' refers to him as 'the scholar of the people of Shām (Greater Syria)'.

However, debate surrounds the exact year of his demise. Historians vary in their accounts, suggesting years ranging from 112 AH to 116 AH as possible dates of his passing. While the exact year is still uncertain, Makḥūl's indelible mark on Islāmic scholarship is undoubted, leaving a legacy that continues to inspire generations.

Mamṭūr Abū Salām al-Ḥabashī

Abū Salām, who later gained renown as Mamṭūr al-Ḥabashī and earned the nickname 'Black-Limbed Damascene', was a significant figure in the world of Islāmic scholarship.

The intriguing journey of Abū Salām begins with his given name, which eventually evolved into his appellation '"Al-Ḥabashī'. It is believed that this nickname stemmed from his lineage to Ethiopia. While the specifics of his ancestry remain unclear, he carved a unique place for himself within the broader context of the Islāmic scholarly tradition. He appeared as a conduit for transmitting the wisdom of the past to the present generation. He is famous for narrating ḥadīth from the luminaries among the the companions of the Prophet ﷺ, such as Ḥudhayfah ibn Al-Yamān, Thawbān, 'Alī ibn Abī Ṭālib, Abū Dharr, and 'Amr ibn 'Abasah, among others. Through them, he became a custodian of the prophetic traditions.

However, Abū Salām's legacy was not confined to merely transmitting narrations; he also had proven connections with the renowned scholars of his time. He absorbed and spread the teachings of esteemed figures such as Abū Umāmah al-Bāhilī, 'Abdur-Raḥmān ibn Ghanm,

Abū Asmā' al-Raḥbī, and more. Abū Salām's journey reached its conclusion between 101-110 AH. His teachings and contributions, notably documented in sources such as 'Siyar A'lām al-Nubālā'' by Shams ad-Dīn Abū 'Abdillāh Muḥammad ibn Aḥmad ibn 'Uthmān ibn Qayyim adh-Dhahabī, continue to resonate through the corridors of Islāmic scholarship. His influence echoes in the hearts and minds of scholars and seekers of knowledge alike, marking him as a luminary whose impact transcends time.

Nāfi' ibn 'Abdur Raḥmān al-Madanī

Nāfi' ibn 'Abdur Raḥmān al-Laithī, an esteemed figure in Black Muslim history, left an indelible mark on the science of Qur'ānic recitation. He served as a mawlā (freedman) of Ja'ūnah ibn Shu'ūb al-Laithī al-Kanānī and gained widespread recognition as one of the ten Qarīs. In the holy city of Madīnah, he held the prestigious position of being the Imām of the Qur'ānic reciters, playing a vital role in preserving and issuing Qur'ānic knowledge.

Nāfi' was born in the region of Isfahān, approximately 70 AH, during the caliphate of 'Abdul Malik ibn Marwān. Tracing his lineage to the people of Madīnah, he belonged to the third generation of Muslims after the companions of the Prophet Muḥammad ﷺ.

Revered by various names, such as 'Abū Ruwaym', 'Abū al-Ḥasan', and 'Abū Nu'aym', Nāfi' had a striking appearance with a dark complexion and a gentle disposition. His exemplary kindness and humility endeared him to his companions.

As the Imām of the Qur'ān, Nāfi' played a significant role in educating and guiding the Tābi'īn. Approximately seventy of them were fortunate to receive intellectual assistance from his teachings. Notable among his students were 'Abdur Raḥmān ibn Ḥārith al-A'raj, Abū Ja'far Yazīd ibn al-Qa'qā', Shaybah ibn Niṣāh, Muslim ibn Jundub al-Hadhlī, and Yazīd ibn Rūmān.

Some of these students also went on to find their own recitation styles, including 'Īsā ibn Mīnā (Qālūn), 'Uthmān ibn Sa'īd (Warsh), 'Īsā ibn Wardān (Ibn Wardān), Sulaymān ibn Jammāz (Ibn Jammāz) and Isḥāq ibn Muḥammad (al-Masībī). In fact, even the great scholar and jurist, Imām Mālik ibn Anas, learned the Qur'ān from Nāfi' and adopted his recitation style in his famous work, 'Al-Muwaṭṭa''. Al-Ḥadīthī noted that Nāfi' devoted approximately ninety-five years to teaching the Qur'ān. His recitation was so well respected that Imām Mālik considered the recitation of Nāfi' to be the Sunnah. Additionally, it is said that when 'Abdullāh ibn Aḥmad ibn Ḥanbal sought his father's opinion on the best recitation, Imām Aḥmad ibn Ḥanbal marked his preference as the recitation of the people of Madīnah, which was synonymous with the recitation of Nāfi'.

Al-Jāḥiẓ

Abū 'Uthmān 'Amr ibn Baḥr ibn Maḥbūb, known as Al-Jāḥiẓ, was born in Baṣrah, present-day Iraq, in approximately 781 AD. His family, of modest means, was very poor. His grandfather was a Black jammāl (cameleer) or ḥammāl (porter), and Al-Jāḥiẓ himself asserted in his own book that he was a member of the Arabian tribe Banū Kinānah. Al-Jāḥiẓ was known for his distinctive physical appearance, particularly his prominent, bulging eyes, a feature that is believed to have inspired his nickname 'Al-Jāḥiẓ', which roughly translates to 'the goggle-eyed' in Arabic. He was also recognised for his jet-black skin, a physical attribute that connected him to a rumoured African ancestry and played a significant role in his identity and writings, particularly his defence of black people's capabilities and virtues in his most famous book 'Fakhr as-Sūdān 'alā al-Bīḍān' (The Superiority of the Blacks to the Whites).

Despite their financial limitations, Al-Jāḥiẓ sought knowledge fervently. He sold fish along one of the canals in Baṣrah to support his family while also gathering with other young learners at Baṣrah's main mosque to discuss various scientific subjects. During the intellectual revolution under the Abbasid Caliphate, books became more accessible, allowing Al-Jāḥiẓ to study philology, lexicography, and poetry under the most learned scholars at the School of Baṣrah. He attended lectures from the likes of Abū

ʿUbaydah, Al-Aṣmaʿī, and Saʿīd ibn Aws al-Anṣārī and studied ʿIlm an-Naḥw (Grammar) with Akhfash al-Awsaṭ. His readings also extended to translated Greek sciences and Hellenistic philosophy, including the works of Aristotle.

His career took a significant turn when he moved to Baghdad, in 816 AD, drawn by the encouragement of scientists and scholars by the caliphs and the foundation of the library of the Bayt al-Ḥikmah. Here, he immersed himself in the intellectual climate, serving as a secretariat of Al-Mȧmūn for a brief three days and, more significantly, as a tutor and intellectual for the city's elite. He was even briefly considered for a position as tutor to the caliph Al-Mȧmūn's children, a plan that was aborted when his distinctively prominent eyes frightened them. His literary talent, sharp wit, vast knowledge, and even his use of marketplace speech attracted attention.

He then moved to Sāmarrā, where he authored a substantial number of his works. Among his many works, which cover a wide range of topics, including theology, biology, social issues, and literature. His most notable work is 'Kitāb al-Ḥayawān' (The Book of Animals) and 'Fakhr as-Sūdān ʿalā al-Bīḍān' (The Superiority of the Blacks to the Whites).

In 'Kitāb al-Ḥayawān' (The Book of Animals), Al-Jāḥiẓ introduces ideas that can be seen as early precursors to some aspects of the theory of evolution. These concepts were introduced more than a thousand years before Charles Darwin's 'On the Origin of Species' (1859). In his work, Al-Jāḥiẓ observes how animals undergo a form of 'struggle for existence', with stronger animals managing to gain advantage and survival over weaker ones. He also noticed how animals adapt to their environments, writing about environmental determinism and guessing about the effects of the environment on the likelihood of an animal's survival.

'Fakhr as-Sūdān 'alā al-Bīḍān' (The Superiority of the Blacks to the Whites) is another notable work by Al-Jāḥiẓ, where he makes an impassioned argument for the intellectual, moral, and physical superiority of blacks over whites. He extols the virtues of the people of the Sūdān (a term generally referring to people of sub-Saharan Africa), citing their physical strength, beauty, bravery, eloquence, and moral virtue. He makes his case using a variety of arguments, drawing upon religious texts, historical events, and the natural world. Al-Jāḥiẓ wrote this text within a societal context in which anti-black discourse and colourism were unfortunately prevalent. During this time, people of African descent were often associated with servitude, due to the trans-Saharan slave trade, and colourism (i.e. discrimination based on skin colour) which was deeply ingrained in society. His arguments challenge these negative stereotypes and prejudices.

Despite the intellectual stimulation of Baghdad and Sāmarrā, Al-Jāḥiẓ eventually returned to Baṣrah, where he lived with his concubine, her maid, a manservant, and a donkey on his estate, and it is there where he spent the last years of his life.

Al-Jāḥiẓ died in 868/869 AD, and while the exact cause of death is unclear, a popular narrative suggests that he met his end in his private library when a large pile of books fell on him.

Dhūn-Nūn al-Miṣrī

Thawbān ibn Ibrāhīm al-Miṣrī, known to many as 'Dhūn-Nūn', was a luminary within the early spiritual traditions of Islām. Born in Akhmim, in Upper Egypt in 796 AD, Dhūn-Nūn came from noble Nubian roots. His honorific 'Dhūn-Nūn', meaning 'the one of the fish', is often associated with the narrative of Prophet Jonah (Yūnus), and is an honorific meant to highlight his spiritual depth and profound gnosis. In his early years, Dhūn-Nūn pursued studies in alchemy, medicine, and Greek philosophy. However, his heart's pull towards spirituality led him to Saʿdūn of Cairo, who became both his mentor and spiritual guide. Following years of spiritual pedagogy, Dhūn-Nūn travelled widely across Arabia and Syria, gaining knowledge and wisdom that he would bring back to his spiritual disciples.

Those journeys eventually led to his greatest trial in 829 AD. Accused of heresy, he was imprisoned in Baghdad. Despite this, his spiritual integrity remained intact. Undeterred, Dhūn-Nūn stood before the Abbasid caliph, Al-Mutawakkil, delivering a spiritual discourse that moved the Caliph to tears. This ultimately led to his release and dignified return to Cairo by the Caliph's order.

It is difficult to overstate Dhūn-Nūn's significance within the early spiritual traditions of Islām. He is often depicted as the spiritual mentor of Sahl at-Tustarī, himself a noted master of the spiritual tradition, who respectfully deferred to Dhūn-Nūn's spiritual discourse, recognising his superior wisdom and gnosis.

Dhūn-Nūn's teachings, captured in sayings and poems, emphasised the path of gnosis (known as 'ma'rifah'), standing alongside love (maḥabbah), and fear (makhāfah), as essential elements of spiritual realisation within Islāmic spirituality. His written works may not have survived, but his wisdom lives on in the vast collection of sayings, poems, and aphorisms attributed to him. Dhūn-Nūn was not only a man of spiritual depth. As an alchemist, he was rumoured to have known the secret of the Egyptian hieroglyphs and had the ability to read and translate them. Dhūn-Nūn was also known to have met Rābi'ah al-'Adawiyyah, a fellow mystic, sharing with her the concept of Divine Love. Their mutual understanding enriched the spiritual traditions of

Islām with a profound exploration of love as a path to Divine realisation.

His life was a testament to his unwavering pursuit of knowledge, his boundless love for the Divine, and his steadfast dedication to the spiritual path, a legacy that endures within the heart of all of Islām's spiritual traditions.

'Alī ibn Riḍwān

Abū al-Ḥasan 'Alī ibn Riḍwān ibn 'Alī ibn Ja'far al-Maṣrī, born in Giza in 988 AD and died in 1061 AD in Cairo, was an Arab physician and astronomer. He was among the prominent physicians, astronomers, and philosophers of his time. He grew up in impoverished surroundings; his father worked as a baker. Thus, he had to work at a young age to support his education.

He mentions about himself, "When I was six years old, I dedicated myself to learning. By the time I reached the age of ten, I moved to the great city (Cairo) and devoted myself to education. When I turned fourteen, I began studying medicine and philosophy. I had limited funds, so I faced challenges in my pursuit of education. I sometimes earned by practising astrology, sometimes through medical practice, and sometimes through teaching."

The physician, Ibn Abī Asyibah, explicitly stated in his biography on 'Alī ibn Riḍwān that 'Alī belonged to the black community. Similarly, Ṣalāḥ ud-Dīn aṣ-Ṣafadi also noted in his biography that Ibn Riḍwān had a black complexion. It is unfortunate that, over time, European depictions have inaccurately portrayed him as having a lighter complexion, contradicting the well-documented Arab historical accounts that describe his physical appearance accurately.

Ibn Riḍwān's prominence in astronomy came after his detailed observation and recording of the most significant astronomical events in recorded history, particularly the supernova of 1006 AD. This event, known as the Great Supernova, occurred on 30th April 1006 AD, and was a massive stellar explosion. It was seen from various parts of the Earth and documented by astronomers in Japan and China. Ibn Riḍwān meticulously described the event when he was just eighteen years old, detailing its size, location, and intensity of brightness compared to Venus and the Moon.

Beyond that, one of Ibn Riḍwān's significant contributions involved his innovations in medicine, namely, his emphasis on the clinical examination of patients. He believed in diagnosing illnesses through observation of the patient's appearance, skin, internal and external organs, speech, gait, and pulse. His work highlighted the importance of understanding the root cause of diseases before trying treatment.

Collectively, he wrote approximately one hundred books and treatises on medicine and philosophy. Of these were commentaries on ancient Greek medicine, particularly on Galen. His commentary on Galen's 'Ars Parva', among other works, was translated by Gerardo Cremonese in 1496. This dissemination of his work would eventually earn him recognition among European authors, who knew him as 'Hali', 'Haly', or 'Haly Abenrudian'.

Hammād at-Tīnātī

Abū al-Khayr al-Aqṭaʿ at-Tīnātī, known by some as Hammād ibn ʿAbdillāh, was a prominent figure in the 4th century AH, distinguished by his unwavering devotion to the Sunnī tradition and his remarkable influence in the realm of spirituality. Known for his dark complexion, he originally hailed from the Maghreb, then settled in Tīnāt (a village near Aleppo) and later, Mount Lebanon. Despite living and travelling throughout the Middle East, Abū al-Khayr remained grounded in his African roots, and intriguingly, he kept the ability to converse fluently in his native language throughout his life.

Although details of his early life are sparse, he was clearly an enigmatic figure who radiated an unparalleled spiritual magnetism. It is said that his unwavering reliance on God's providence not only resonated with humans but also attracted the wild creatures of the land. Abū al-Khayr al-Aqṭaʿ at-Tīnātī's legacy echoed through the annals of Ṣūfī history. His teachings found eager receptivity among his disciples, guiding the next generations along the path of devotion and self-purification. His remarkable life journey illuminated the essence of unwavering faith and a profound connection to the divine realm.

His son, ʿĪsā, narrated from him, where he said, "I was a black slave, and my heart felt constricted in servitude. Therefore, I supplicated to Allāh, and He granted me freedom. I travelled to Alexandria, where I would buy and sell to sustain myself. I used to enter the mosque and stand at the back, aware that they did not recognise me as I was a black slave. I would stand there and Allāh would ease the speech of the people around me, allowing me to ask what I intended. One day, I heard the story of Prophet Yaḥyā ibn Zakariyyā and what was done to him (his body being amputated). I thought to myself, if Allāh had tested me with something in my body, I should be patient. I then went to the frontier in Ṭarṭūs, carrying lawful provisions, a shield, and a sword. I fought the enemies in a war alongside the people. At night, I entered the cave, not knowing that the road had been cut off by robbers, and they entered the cave ahead of me. When I went inside, the chief of police was looking for them, and he found them. They captured me along with them.

When they arrived, the robbers said, "This black man was not with us." The people of the area knew me, but

Allāh concealed me from them until they cut my hand. After that, it was as if a veil was lifted from them and they recognised me, saying, "This is Abū al-Khayr", and they were amazed.

When they intended to immerse my severed hand in oil, I resisted. I left and entered the cave, spending a long night. I fell asleep and saw the Prophet ﷺ in my dream. I said, "Oh Messenger of Allāh, they have done this to me." He took my severed hand and kissed it. When I woke up, I found no pain from the wound and it had healed."

Abū al-Khayr also narrated himself, "I entered the city of the Messenger of Allāh ﷺ, while I was in poverty. I stayed for five days without tasting proper food. Then, I approached the grave and greeted the Prophet ﷺ, as well as Abū Bakr and ʿUmar, may Allāh be pleased with them. I said, "I am your guest tonight, Oh Messenger of Allāh." I stepped aside and slept behind the pulpit. In my dream, I saw the Prophet ﷺ with Abū Bakr on his right side, ʿUmar on his left side, and ʿAlī ibn Abī Ṭālib in front of him, may Allāh be pleased with them. The Prophet ﷺ moved me forward and said, "Stand up, for the Messenger of Allāh has come." Therefore, I stood up and approached him. I kissed between his eyes, and he handed me a piece of bread. I ate half of it, then I became aware and found the other half in my hand."

Artists

Sa'īd bn Misjaḥ

Abū 'Uthmān Sa'īd ibn Misjaḥ al-Makkī was one of the early Arab singers in Makkah and the Ḥijāz. He was born in the 7th century AD / 1st century AH and died in the early 8th century. He was known for his pioneering role in Arab singing, such that the next generations of singers were influenced by him. He was a slave belonging to the Banū Nawfal ibn Al-Ḥārith ibn 'Abdil Muṭṭalib, or it was said that he belonged to the Banū Makhzūm or the Banū Jumaḥ. Sa'īd ibn Misjaḥ was very dark skinned. He was intelligent and witty, leaving his master impressed by him.

In his youth, his master would say, "This boy will have a great future. The only thing that prevents me from freeing him is my astuteness in him. If I live, I will see that, and if I die, he will be a free man." One day, his master heard him singing a poem by Ibn ar-Ruqā' al-'Āmilī and was so impressed with his voice and the innovative style in which he sang the poem that he called him and said, "O my son, repeat to me what I heard from you." He repeated it, and his repetition of it better than when he had initially sung it. His master asked, "How did you come up with this (way of singing)?" He replied, "I heard these foreigners singing in Persian, so I grasped it and sang this poem in the same way." His master said to him, "For the sake of God, you are free."

He stayed in the company of his master; however, his singing flourished and the people of Makkah admired him for his talent and the beauty of his voice. He gained a reputation for being able to adapt melodies from neighbouring artistic cultures and present them in a new Arabic form. An-Nuwayrī says, "Singing existed in Persia and Rome before the Arabs had anything, other than hadda and nashīd, which they called 'Ar-Rukbāniyyah'. The first person to introduce Persian singing to the Arabs of Makkah was Saʿīd ibn Misjaḥ."

Interestingly, his first exposure to foreign musical elements was when he heard Persian workers singing their Persian songs whilst they were building and renovating the Kaʿbah during the reign of ʿAbdullāh ibn Zubayr. It was also said that he heard them when they were constructing the famous houses of Muʿāwiyah in Makkah. From those songs and melodies, he took what he saw fit and sang them. However, he did not stop there. Historical sources mention that he also embarked on a journey to the Levant and took melodies from the Byzantine Romans and their neighbours. Then, he travelled to Persia and took many melodies also from there.

He learned to play instruments and returned to the Ḥijāz after refining and polishing the singing techniques he had brought. He presented them in a way that resonated with the Arab ears and tastes. As a result of his original style and fame, he established his own musical school, which later singers from the Ḥijāz and other regions followed and benefitted from his techniques.

Of his notable students was Ibn Sarīj al-Mughannī, who was also a slave. In fact, they had both belonged to the same master. After their master freed Ibn Sarīj and emancipated him, he asked that Ibn Misjaḥ teach and train Ibn Sarīj in the art of singing. Their master said to Ibn Misjaḥ, "My son, teach him and dedicate yourself to him." Ibn Sarīj had a remarkable voice and learned from Ibn Misjaḥ, eventually becoming renowned in his own right.

Historical sources do not supply a specific date for the death of Sa'īd ibn Misjaḥ. However, Abū al-Faraj al-Isfahānī mentions in his book 'Al-Aghānī' that he lived until he met Ma'bad al-Mughannī and learned from him. This meeting took place during the reign of Walīd ibn 'Abdul Malik in the early 8th century AD. Nevertheless, although the exact details of his life and death may not be extensively documented, his contributions to the field of Arab singing are recognised and remembered.

'Alī ibn Nāfi'' Ziryāb'

Abū al-Ḥasan 'Alī ibn Nāfi', more commonly known as 'Ziryāb', graced the world of medieval Andalusia with his unique artistry. Born approximately 789 AD in Baghdad, his journey as a polymath, musician, fashion influencer, and culinary pioneer unfolded across multiple regions and earned him a place of honour in history. Ziryāb's fascination with music blossomed at a tender age; his innate talent was clear to all who heard him.

His journey began under the esteemed Persian musician, Ibrāhīm al-Mawṣilī, in Baghdad, a city pulsating with musical vibrancy. However, Ziryāb's identity and heritage remains a matter of scholarly discussion. The prevailing belief is that he hailed from Africa, as suggested by Ibn Ḥayyān. It was his deeply dark complexion that earned him the nickname 'Blackbird', based not only on his physical appearance but also on the clarity of his voice and the sweetness of his character.

However, Ziryāb's journey took him far from Baghdad's musical heart. During the Abbasid era, he embarked on an expedition that ultimately led him to Córdoba in Al-Andalus, in modern day Spain. It was there that he found a new home under the patronage of 'Abdur Raḥmān II, the prince of the Umayyad Dynasty.

Ziryāb's musical prowess blossomed in the vibrant court of 'Abdur Raḥmān II. Ziryāb had learned the intricacies of the oud, a precursor to the modern guitar, in Baghdad. His innovative spirit led him to expand the oud's capabilities, adding a pair of strings and adopting an eagle's quill as a plectrum. This transformation resulted in an instrument of more depth and resonance, enhancing his performance.

Within the splendid halls of 'Abdur Raḥmān II's court, Ziryāb's influence was profound. He established one of the first schools of music in Córdoba, welcoming male and female students who captivated the aristocracy with their performances. Ziryāb's artistry and affability earned him a monthly salary of 200 Gold Dinars, certifying his status as an esteemed member of the court. His connection with 'Abdur Raḥmān II was deep-rooted, and he also enjoyed a close companionship with the prince. This intimacy allowed Ziryāb to exert his influence in various aspects of courtly life, including fashion, grooming, music, and gastronomy. His teachings resonated through generations, shaping the court's cultural legacy for years to come.

Beyond his musical virtuosity, Ziryāb's influence spanned a vast spectrum of domains. His impact in the realm of fashion was monumental. He set remarkable trends by adapting his attire choices to various weather conditions and seasons. He advocated for different clothing styles during the morning, afternoon, and evening hours, as well as different types of clothes for different seasons.

In the context of hairstyling, Ziryāb's impact was equally remarkable. According to historical sources, before his influence, men and women in Al-Andalus, particularly within the Cordoban court, wore their hair long and parted in the middle, flowing freely toward their shoulders. Ziryāb, however, adopted a distinct hairstyle featuring straight-cut bangs that graced his eyebrows, inspiring members of the court to opt for shorter hairstyles that exposed their neck and ears. Furthermore, he also improved hair care practices by introducing fragrant oils and salt, leaving from the previously prevalent use of rose water.

His contributions to self-care also extended to the broader realm of personal hygiene. He pioneered a unique deodorant solution to counteract unpleasant odours and emphasised the significance of regular morning and evening baths. Additionally, he introduced a toothpaste precursor in Islāmic Iberia, a product that was reportedly both effective and pleasing in taste. He also inspired new shaving practices among the court's men.

As a tastemaker and culinary pioneer, he also revolutionised local food culture by introducing novel fruits and vegetables such as asparagus. He was the one who invented and advocated for the adoption of the three-course meal; elegantly served on leather tablecloths. This new approach divided meals into distinct courses—soup/starter, a main dish, and dessert, which was never known in Europe before, all of which was to be served alongside crystal containers for beverages, a departure from conventional metal vessels and a precursor to the glasses we use today. Ziryāb's legacy surpassed the confines of his lifetime. Through his melodies, sartorial sensibilities, grooming practices, and culinary advancements, he left an imprint on the canvas of medieval Andalusia. As the innovations he introduced into Andalusia spread across Europe, Ziryāb's legacy also directly influenced modern Western culture. His contributions to music, fashion, grooming, and gastronomy shaped various aspects of contemporary society. Ziryāb's enhancement of the oud and development of distinct musical styles are what directly influenced modern Western music. His revolutionary ideas in fashion, adaptation of attire to weather, season and occasions resonate in the core principles of modern fashion trends. His transformation of dining experiences, introduction of three-course meals, and emphasis on presentation continue to shape modern culinary culture. It seems that much of the Western world's innovations have their origins in the creativity of this Black, Afro-Arab, Muslim man - Ziryāb.

Rulers

Abū al-Misk Kāfūr al-Ikhshīdī

From the depths of servitude to the pinnacles of power, the life story of Abū al-Misk Kāfūr is a testament to his unparalleled perseverance and extraordinary abilities. He was born in the 10th century AD in the province of Lab in Nubia, southern Egypt. According to the biographical dictionary of Ibn Khallikān, he had a deep black colour.

Enslaved, Kāfūr's first years were marked by hardship. That was until he caught the eye of Muḥammad ibn Tughj, the founder of the Ikhshīdid dynasty of Egypt, who, after buying him for eighteen pieces of gold, saw in him a spark of brilliance and rewarded him with freedom. Kāfūr's rise within the Ikhshīdid dynasty was as impressive as it was swift. Ibn Tughj initially appointed him as the supervisor of his sons' education. Eventually, his responsibilities expanded to include military command and diplomatic duties, notably, the exchanges between the Ikhshīdids and the Caliph of Baghdad.

Following the death of Ibn Tughj, Kāfūr became the de facto ruler of Egypt in 946 AD, supporting the façade of Ikhshīdid rule while managing the state's affairs. His rule was just and moderate, despite satirical criticism from Al-Mutanabbī', a renowned Arab poet of his time. At the height of his powers, he ruled not only Egypt and the Ḥijāz (in present-day Saudi Arabia) but also Syria. Public prayers were offered for him in the mosques of Makkah, Cairo, and Damascus. This rule stretched from 946 AD until his death in 968 AD, when he was buried next to the Ikhshīdid emirs in Jerusalem.

Despite the enormous pressure of ruling, Kāfūr managed to keep stability within Egypt, skilfully resolving internal political issues and defending its borders. He successfully protected the Ikhshīdid establishment against external threats from the Ḥamdānids, Fāṭimids, Qarmaṭians, and Nubians, ensuring the survival of the Ikhshīdid dynasty despite the socio-political turmoil that surrounded it. Economically, he also navigated through significant setbacks, including a devastating fire, a major earthquake, and recurrent food-price inflation. He weathered all of these, whilst refraining from heavy taxation.

Kāfūr was a renowned patron of the arts and scholars, fostering a thriving intellectual environment in his court. Before it soured, he enjoyed a brief friendship with Al-Mutanabbī', whose poetic prowess - despite his critical works - served to immortalise Kāfūr's rule. Kāfūr played an instrumental role in fostering an environment that allowed Al-Mutanabbī''s genius to flourish.

Al-Ḥussein ibn Salamah An-Nūbī

Abū 'Abdillāh Al-Ḥussein ibn Salamah An-Nūbī was born into slavery before his life took an extraordinary trajectory, and he rose to become the leader of the Ziyādid Emirate, a medieval Islāmic state that existed in the southern region of the Arabian Peninsula, specifically in parts of present-day Yemen, during the 11th and 12th centuries AD. It was a relatively short-lived dynasty that played a significant role in the political and cultural landscape of the region.

The Ziyādid Emirate was founded by 'Alī ibn Muḥammad al-Ziyādī in the year 1018 AD. He proved his rule in the city of Zabīd, which became the capital of the emirate. The Ziyādids were known for their independent and assertive stance, often resisting the influence of larger neighbouring powers, such as the Fāṭimid Caliphate and the Ṣulayḥid Dynasty.

Under the rule of the Ziyādids, Zabīd flourished as a centre of trade, learning, and culture. The emirate received help from its strategic location along major trade routes that connected East Africa, the Arabian Peninsula, and the Indian Ocean. This assisted the exchange of goods, ideas, and knowledge.

Al-Ḥussein ibn Salamah was a formidable warrior known for his loyalty to the ruling Banī Ziyād dynasty and his strategic prowess, and as his name 'An-Nūbī' suggests, his ancestry originated from the Nubia region in modern-day Sudan. His leadership journey took a pivotal turn following the passing of his predecessor, 'Abdullāh ibn Isḥāq. At that juncture, the once-steady grip of the ruling authorities weakened, allowing local fortress and mountain governors to assert their influence.

Seising the opportunity, Al-Ḥussein assumed the reins of power in the year 375 AH (985 AD). With a visionary approach, he not only set up the foundations of his emirate but also embarked on a mission to quell internal dissensions. His leadership bore fruit as the entire Yemen region coalesced under his banner.

Renowned for his fair and virtuous character, Al-Ḥussein drew comparisons to the esteemed 'Umar ibn 'Abdil 'Azīz. Notable feats in his reign included the capture of strategic locations such as the city of Al-Kidrah along the Suhaym Valley, the Al-Ma'āfira city (also referred to as Al-

Qaḥmah), and ʿUmar al-ʿAqabah (Kura), a key point between Makkah and Ṭā'if. His architectural endeavours displayed his dedication to progress.

ʿUmārah al-Yamānī's testament echoes his monumental impact, where he said "He spearheaded the construction of grand mosques and towering minarets spanning from Haḍramawt to Makkah (covering a vast expanse of sixty days). His legacy extends to wells and tunnels in the Mafawiz area, leaving an indelible mark on history."

An-Nūbī's reign spanned a commendable three decades. Despite his origins and the era's prevalent racial biases, An-Nūbī was a paragon of competence, vision, and unwavering integrity. He was deeply committed to his emirate's unity and independence, ardently opposing any attempts at annexation.

His era marked a significant awakening in Islāmic Yemen's history, characterised by cultural prosperity, political unity, internal stability, and widespread urbanisation. Under his stewardship, Yemen underwent extensive infrastructural and societal changes. His reign also saw the restoration and building of many mosques and congregational spaces. Today, his name is immortalised in these structures across Yemen and the Arabian Peninsula.

Notably, his interest was not limited to architectural endeavours; he was deeply involved in facilitating Ḥajj pilgrimage coordination. He meticulously cared for the trade route connecting the city of Aden with Makkah, ensuring its accessibility for pilgrims. His vision extended to the establishment of many fresh wells along the Yemenī Ḥajj routes; the mountain, central, and coastal paths, and even in Makkah itself, ensuring the comfort of the pilgrims.

The Kings of Āl Najāḥ

After the death of the last Ziyādid king, the guardianship of the child king was assumed by Al-Ḥussein ibn Salamah. His rule saved the Ziyādid Dynasty from total collapse, recovering the original borders of the Kingdom, extending from Haly to Aden, but started a multi decade drama of shifting powers, war, and courtly intrigue. As vizier, Al-Ḥussein appointed two Abyssinian slaves, Nafīs and Najāḥ, as administrators.

Tragedy struck when Nafīs killed the child king, ending the Arab dynasty of Banū Ziyād. After learning of Nafīs' actions, Najāḥ killed Nafīs in 1050 AD (or 1022 AD, according to some sources), paving the way for the Najāḥid Dynasty. Najāḥ, the founder of the Najāḥid Dynasty and a member of the ancient Abyssinian tribe called 'Jazal', ruled with a strong hand. His rule was marked by attempts at unifying the region, although his Abyssinian slave origin led to resistance among tribal elements in Yemen. However, his efforts were not entirely fruitless. Although he lost Aden to the Banū Maʿn Dynasty, he supported some control over the Zabīd region.

Nonetheless, a decade later, ʿAlī aṣ-Ṣulayḥī, founder of the Ismāʿīlī Shīʿa dynasty, conquered Zabīd, killing Najāḥ and forcing his sons to flee, two of whom committed suicide. One, however, said Al-Aḥwal was able to survive and ambushed ʿAlī aṣ-Ṣulayḥī, killing him. Al-Aḥwal was later defeated and fled before his brother, Jayyāsh, returned to Zabīd in 1089 AD, ruling securely until his demise in 1104 AD.

Jayyāsh was succeeded by his son, Al-Fātik, but family disputes led to his death in 1106 AD. His successor, Manṣūr, ruled as a vassal of the Ṣulayḥids in Zabīd, but with the peaceful death of Manṣūr in 1130 AD and the later death of his son, Al-Fātik II, after three years, the dynasty came to an end.

The decline of the Najāḥid dynasty culminated with the rise of the Mahdid dynasty in Tihāmah. The brutal actions of ʿAlī ibn Mahdī al-Ḥimyarī, including the killing of Abyssinians, led to desperation among the people of Zabīd. The execution of Al-Fātik III marked the definitive end of the slave dynasty, and the Mahdids took over Zabīd in 1158 AD.

Despite its dramatic history, the Najāḥid Dynasty established by Najāḥ, who was one of the Abyssinian slaves serving the Ziyādid dynasty, marked the first and only hereditary black slave ruling house in Yemen. Supported by the Abyssinians who adopted Arabic culture, the Najāḥids unified under a strong racial identity. Their legacy was complex and intertwined with both pride and prejudice. As late as the 16th century AD, they were referred to as "abīd' (slaves) in the Yemenī chronicles, ambiguously defining both their ethnic and social position.

As we reflect on the historical contributions of these Afro and Black Arabs, we are confronted with a glaring realisation; these voices and accomplishments have often been obscured or minimised in contemporary discourse. However, the dedication of renowned scholars, such as Al-Jāḥiẓ, Ibn Jawzī, and Imām Suyūṭī, in documenting and celebrating the virtues of Sudanese and Abyssinian peoples underscores the importance of recognising their influence. Their intellectual, revolutionary, and religious contributions shaped the Islāmic tradition and the broader Arab and Muslim world.

The resonance of the Zanj Rebellion echoes through history a powerful testament to their indomitable spirit through history. Their impact, spanning the pre-Islāmic Jāhilī era, the time of Prophet Muḥammad ﷺ, and the Middle Ages, reverberates in the annals of Islāmic empires. The Muftīs of Makkah and Egypt, as well as the foremost scholars of the Levant and the Princes and commanders of Yemen, whose origins trace back to these lands, laid the groundwork for religious and legal discourse, and their influence extended far beyond their lifetimes.

Not confined to religious circles, Sudan and Zanj nurtured an array of intellectuals who excelled across various domains. Their contributions spanned fields as diverse as philosophy, mathematics, astronomy, medicine, and literature, leaving an indelible imprint on the intellectual fabric of Islāmic and later global civilisation. Their work fostered innovation and exchange, igniting a culture of exploration that defined an era.

This invites us to contemplate a richer, more inclusive narrative that pays homage to the invaluable legacy of black Muslims in Middle Eastern Islāmic History. Just as the scholars of old recognised the profound impact of these people, we too must elevate their stories, drawing inspiration from their enduring dedication to the growth of knowledge, the propagation of faith, and the advancement of humanity. By embracing their history, we not only honour their contributions but also enrich our understanding of the interconnected tapestry that is the Islāmic world.

Chapter 5:

AFRICANS IN ASIA; THE SIDDĪS

In 2018, Tanzeela Qambrani, a Pakistani female politician, created history by winning a seat in the Provincial Assembly of Sindh, Pakistan. Her election not only gained national attention but also garnered global recognition. Qambrani, a remarkable figure with her hair elegantly wrapped with a stylish turban, had dark skin and distinct African features that diverged from the stereotypical image of a Pakistani woman. Her ground-breaking achievement extended beyond gender barriers, as she became the first woman from the marginalised 'Sheedī' community to secure a position in the provincial assembly.

The Sheedī community, unbeknownst to most people both inside and outside the country, consists of individuals of African descent in Pakistan. After her election, hundreds of videos appeared on various social media platforms trying to discover who these African people in Asia were, how long they had been there, and how they arrived. To the surprise of many, not only was there a significant African presence in the Asian subcontinent, but as we will explore in this chapter, Qambrani was not the first of the Sheedīs to buy social and political influence in the region.

As we can have learned from the earlier chapters, trade between East Africa and the Middle East has a long history, predating the rise of Islām by many centuries. With the rise of Islām in the 7th century AD, these trade connections took on a new religious and cultural dimension. Muslim merchants, scholars, and missionaries began to travel more often to East Africa, bringing with them the teachings of Islām. In return, many East Africans began to adopt Islām and to integrate more fully into the Islāmic world. The Islāmic expansion, which also extended to parts of the Asian subcontinent, created an interconnected network of trade and religious ties that spanned three continents.

East Africans found themselves not only trading with the Middle East and Asia but also travelling there for study, pilgrimage, and other purposes. Over time, a significant East African diaspora community developed in Asia, particularly in what is now India and Pakistan. This diaspora community is known today as the 'Sheedī' or 'Siddī' community. Their ancestors were merchants, sailors, slaves, and travellers from East Africa who settled in South Asia from the 7th century AD onwards. Over time, their presence gave rise to an ethnic group with a unique culture that blends elements of African, Indian, and Islāmic traditions.

It is important to note, however, that not all Siddīs are descendants of voluntary migrants. The Indian Ocean slave trade, which lasted from the 7th to the 19th centuries AD, forcibly transported many people from East Africa to the Middle East and South Asia. The descendants of these slaves also form part of the Siddī community.

Despite their long presence, the Sheedī community's history and existence are little recognised both within and outside South Asia. This is due to a variety of factors, much, of course, based on the fact that Siddīs faced social, economic, and political marginalisation in South Asian societies. They often live in remote or rural areas where they are disproportionately affected by poverty. Their distinct African heritage and practices have also subjected them to discrimination and prejudice, culturally isolating them from wider subcontinent society.

Additionally, they are underrepresented in media, politics, and popular culture in South Asia. That lack of visibility coupled with - until recently - the disinterest in their study by the academic world, has left the Siddīs overshadowed by other historical and cultural narratives. Finally, another important factor that must not be overlooked is anti-Blackness, a form of prejudice that has roots in historical systems of racism and colourism. Anti-

Blackness refers to specific kinds of racial prejudices directed towards Black individuals or communities, which often manifest in the form of discrimination, social exclusion, or negative stereotypes. Although the precise forms of anti-Blackness can vary from one cultural context to another, it is a global phenomenon and is not limited to Western societies. In the context of South Asia, anti-Blackness can be linked to colourism; a bias that favours lighter skin tones over darker ones, which is deeply entrenched in many aspects of society, from beauty standards to social status. Despite South Asia's diversity of skin tones and ethnicities, darker skin is often associated with lower social status, and this bias can contribute to the discrimination faced by Siddīs due to their African heritage.

Trade & Travel

The history of East Africans in South Asia can be traced back to the time of Ḥajjāj ibn Yūsuf, a key figure in the Umayyad Empire, who governed Iraq from 661 AD to 714 AD. Ḥajjāj's service under Caliph ʿAbdul Malik (r. 685 AD –705 AD) saw him rise through the ranks to become the head of the Caliph's shurṭah (select troops). Further promotions followed, with Ḥajjāj appointed as the governor of the Ḥijāz (western Arabia) from 692 AD to 694 AD and later serving as the practical viceroy of a unified Iraqī province and the eastern parts of the Caliphate starting in 694 AD. Even under the reign of ʿAbdul Malik's son and successor, Al-Walīd I (r. 705 AD – 715 AD), Ḥajjāj kept his influential post, helping shape decisions until his demise in 714 AD.

In his quest to expand the empire's influence, Ḥajjāj dispatched three expeditions to Sind, now a part of modern-day Pakistan. Despite the first failures, the third mission — forming a large force of East African regiments under the command of Ḥajjāj's son-in-law and nephew, Muḥammad ibn Qāsim — achieved significant success. These East Africans, owing to their unique combat strategies and military prowess, eased Muslim victories over Hindu armies, marking the commencement of East African presence in the region.

Next, conflicts and wars in East Africa resulted in the capture of prisoners of war who were then exported to the Arab world and from there, to the Islāmicised regions of South Asia. As the historian, Pankhurst, points out, roughly an average of 25,000 individuals, including slaves, traders, immigrants, and indentured labourers, migrated from East Africa to South Asia annually. These turbulent periods in East Africa and the resulting mass movements of people are well documented, and the arrival of these diverse groups has indelibly contributed to the cultural, economic, and societal landscapes of South Asia.

The history of the East African presence in the Indian subcontinent is, therefore, vibrant and nuanced, dating back centuries. Richard F. Burton, a British colonial scholar, soldier, and traveller, once described Berbera, Somalia, as "The emporium of India," emphasising the significant trade connection between the horn of Africa and the Asian Sub-Continent. Meanwhile, British historian Denison Ross highlighted that, "From the end of the 13th century to the end of the 17th century, soldiers, traders, and slaves kept flocking into Gujarāt by land and sea." His close study of Gujarāt's history in the 15th and 16th centuries AD led him to critique European historians for their failure to attach sufficient importance to the role played by the Ḥabashīs (East Africans) in the history of India.

The 13th-century Venetian traveller Marco Polo noted the military prowess of the province of Ḥabash, who sourced many of the soldiers in their army from East Africa, declaring that, "There are excellent soldiers and many horsemen. They have a great number of horses and soldiers in all the provinces of India." Likewise, the famed explorer, Ibn Baṭṭūṭah, during his visit to India from 1334-1342 AD, remarked on the presence of East Africans, notably a Ḥabashī governor named Badr, whose courage had become proverbial. These individuals, originally known as Ḥabashīs (a term derived from the Arabic word Ḥabash, denoting the residents of the Horn of Africa), played a crucial role in keeping safety on the Indian Ocean. As told in 'The African Dispersal in the Deccan: From Medieval to Modern

Times,’, it is mentioned that, “Let there be but one of them on a ship, and it will be avoided by the Indian pirates and idolaters.”

Interestingly, the term ‘“Siddī”’, a corruption of the Arabic word Sayyid or ‘Master’, was once an honorific title for East African captains who transported goods and people to South Asia. Over time, the terms ‘Ḥabashī’ and ‘Siddī’ became synonymous with Africans or Blacks in South Asia. Historically, the Siddīs have occupied a wide range of roles within South Asian societies, reflecting the diverse circumstances under which they arrived in the region and the socio-political contexts they met.

Economically, they contributed as artisans, craftsmen, and labourers across a range of industries, from construction to textile production. Siddīs enriched the cultural fabric of South Asia, bringing with them distinct music, dance, and other cultural practices, such as Goma music and dance tradition, both of which have African roots. Many Siddīs, distinguished for their physical prowess and military skills, also served as soldiers, guards, or mercenaries in local armies.

Their presence was notably felt in elite military units, and some, such as the renowned 16th-17th century AD military leader Mālik ‘Ambar, even rose to significant positions of leadership. In addition to their military roles, Siddīs were key figures in maritime activities, using their navigational skills and deep understanding of the Indian Ocean trade routes to serve in the naval fleets of various coastal states.

Some Siddīs achieved prominence in courtly roles, rising to positions of administration and governance, most notably in regions such as Janjira and Sachin in Western India, where they set up their own states.

Tārīkh Gujurāt

Shaykh 'Abdullāh Muḥammad ibn 'Umar al-Makkī, also known more popularly as 'Al-Ḥājjī ad-Dabīr', is a significant figure in the narrative of East Africans in South Asia. He began his career in the service of two Ḥabashī noblemen of Gujarāt, specifically Muḥammad Yāqūt Ulugh Khān and later, 'Abdul Karīm Sayfūd Muḥammad Fūkad Khān, in the 1500s. Al-Ḥājjī ad-Dabīr then went on to write an Arabic history of Gujarāt titled 'Ẓafar al-Wālih bi-Muẓaffar wa ālihī' ("The Excellent Victories of Muẓaffar and his family"), also known as 'Tārīkh Gujurāt'.

These writings shed light on conflicts dating back to the 12th century AD, which resulted in the large-scale displacement of East Africans. Initially, these prisoners of war were sent from their homeland to Arabia, where Amīr Salmān of Zabīd undertook their education and training. Upon his murder in 1529 AD, his nephew, Muṣṭafā ibn Bahrām, took over and handled sending the now well-prepared army to aid Gujarāt's Sulṭān Bahādur Shāh (r. 1526-1537 AD) against formidable Portuguese forces.

Notably, a mere year after the East Africans arrived to bolster Sulṭān Bahādur Shāh's ranks in 1530 CE, an African named Sayf al-Mulk Miftāḥ ascended to the role of commander and governor of Dāmāt Fort, leading a force of 4,000 of his fellow countrymen. As Al-Ḥājjī ad-Dabīr poignantly writes in 'Tarikh Gujurāt', "It was in this manner that these Ḥabashīs came to Gujurāt and the manner in which many of them rose to prominence and independence forms one of the most interesting features of this story." This remark, found in E. Denison Ross's "An Arabic History of Gujarat Vol I", succinctly encapsulates the fascinating journey of East Africans from their origins to their newfound homes and their later ascension within South Asian societies.

Jamāl ad-Dīn Yāqūt

Jamāl ad-Dīn Yāqūt, the first Ḥabashī, or East African, recorded by name in the history of the Asian subcontinent, is etched into the annals of time due to his integral role in the rise and reign of Sulṭān Raḍiyyah, known as Razia Sultan. As the first and only female monarch of the Delhi Sultanate in India, Razia's reign from 1236 AD to 1240 AD marked a significant shift in power dynamics. Razia, the daughter of Sultan Shams ud-Dīn Īltutmish, the third ruler of the Delhi Sultanate, was chosen by her father as his successor, bypassing his sons. This decision was based on Razia's proven skills in governance, intellectual prowess, and ability in military and administrative matters. Īltutmish, convinced of Razia's competence, once proclaimed, "[My] sons give themselves up to wine, and every other excess and none of them possesses the capability of managing the affairs of the country. Raḍiyyah was better than twenty such sons."

Minhāj-i-Sirāj Juzjānī, a 13th-century Persian historian born in the region of Ghur, was the principal historian for the Mamlūk Sultanate of Delhi in northern India. He noted, "Sulṭān Raḍiyyah was a great monarch. She was wise, just and generous. A benefactor to her kingdom, a dispenser of justice, the protector of her subjects, and the leader of her armies. She was endowed with all the qualities befitting a king." Intriguingly, Juzjānī used the masculine form of her title, signifying the strength of her reign. However, he ended his assessment with a stark indictment of the societal norms of the time, saying, "However, she was not born of the right sex, and so in the estimation of men, all these virtues were worthless."

Raḍiyyah faced her first test of leadership when her half-brother Fīrawz, backed by his mother, rebelled against her. In response, she made a successful appeal to the army and the people, resulting in Fīrawz's capture and execution in November 1236 AD. From then on, she firmly proved her authority, attentively hearing out the grievances of her subjects, from the crowds in the marketplace to the poor and the destitute, and dispensing justice.

Raḍiyyah was a fearless leader. As Ibn Baṭṭūṭah puts it, "She ruled as an absolute monarch [and] mounted a horse like a man, armed with bow and quiver, and without veiling her face." In her role as the military commander, she personally led the army, effectively crushed rebellions and quelled insurgencies. She kept the Mongols at bay with her clever negotiations. Notably, she had coins minted with inscriptions of "Commander of the Faithful" and "Most Mighty Sulṭān."

Yāqūt, blessed with good looks and an affable personality, became an influential figure in the Sulṭānah's court, aggravating the Turkic nobles' resentment. The atmosphere in her court shifted dramatically when she appointed Jamāl ad-Dīn Yāqūt to the prestigious post of the Sulṭānah's equerry - a position that entailed the care of the royal horses and involved proximity to the Sulṭānah. The disgruntled Turkish slaves and lords at court, in turn, spread rumours about the nature of the relationship between Yāqūt and the queen, citing 'a very great degree of familiarity' between them, as one contemporary historian noted.

The potent favour of Razia bestowed upon Jamāl ad-Dīn Yāqūt marked a significant shift in the political dynamics of her court. Razia's decision to award Yāqūt the honorific titles of 'Amīr al-Khayl' (Commander of Horses) and later the higher rank of 'Amīr al-Umarā'' (Commander of Commanders) was received with consternation and outrage by the Turkic nobility. Already challenged for being a female ruler in the Muslim kingdom, Razia's close association with an Abyssinian slave, considered racially inferior by the ruling Turkic nobles, added fuel to the growing discontent.

Rumours about an alleged affair between Razia and Yāqūt were circulated, with many historians arguing that these were deliberate falsehoods orchestrated by the disgruntled nobles to trigger her downfall. This brewing discontent eventually erupted in an open rebellion led by Mālik Ikhtiyār ud-Dīn Altūniyā, the governor of Bhātīndā. Anticipating a siege, Razia and Yāqūt left Delhi to confront the rebels but faced defeat. In the ensuing battle, Yāqūt was killed, and Razia was captured, imprisoned at Bhātīndā by Altūniyā, and later married. The once powerful queen, along with her new husband, met her end in a battle against her stepbrother, Mu'izz ud-Dīn Bahrām, who had usurped the throne of Delhi in Razia's absence.

The life of Razia Sultan has indeed captivated filmmakers and audiences alike, with many cinematic adaptations. Among the earliest portrayals was 'Razia Begum' (1924), an Indian silent film directed by Nanubhai B. Desai and Bhagwati Prasad Mishra. This was followed by 'Razia

Sultana' (1961), an Indian Hindi-language film by Devendra Goel, featuring Nirupa Roy in the title role. More contemporary takes include the 1983 biopic 'Razia Sultan' by Kamal Amrohi, with Hema Malini donning the lead character, and the 2015 TV series 'Razia Sultan', with Pankhuri Awasthy and Rohit Purohit as Razia and Altūniyā, respectively. In 2016, Rachel Gill portrayed a character inspired by the empress in the Pakistani film 'Sayā e Khudā e Zuljalāl.'

Despite these diverse representations of Razia Sultan's life, it is lamentable that the portrayal of Jamāl ad-Din Yāqūt has often been either overlooked or misinterpreted. Often, Yāqūt is not depicted as the historically black African that he was, if he is even depicted at all. Biases can undoubtedly distort historical narratives and representation in media, leading to the whitewashing of historically black figures or their outright exclusion. Such erasure not only serves to perpetuate damaging stereotypes but also denies the rich diversity and complexity of our shared history. Recognising and challenging these biases is critical to fostering more exact historical narratives.

Bilāl Jhujhar Khān Ḥabashī

Bilāl Jhujhar Khān Ḥabashī was another East African who served as the governor of Burhānpūr, now in Madhya Pradesh, from 1538 AD to 1539 AD. His appointment came during the reign of Mubārak Shāh of Khāndesh, reflecting the significant trust and responsibility bestowed upon him. Bilāl's life, however, met a premature end as he fell in battle near the thriving commercial town of S'rat in 1558-9 AD. As a mark of respect and honour, he was buried in Sarkhej, signifying his prestige and influence. However, his impact did not cease with his demise. Bilāl's lineage continued to shape the course of history in Gujarāt. His son, 'Azīz Khān, and later his grandson, Amīn Khān, appeared as influential figures, echoing the significance of their Ḥabashī family in the region.

Mandal Dilāwar Khān Ḥabashī

Mandal Dilāwar Khān Ḥabashī, also known as Ulugh Khān I, originating from the region of East Africa, was amongst the early Africans to have journeyed to the Indian subcontinent amid ongoing conflicts in his homeland. Dilāwar Khān gained the distinction of being the first African to receive the illustrious title 'Ulugh Khān'. He was a trusted confidant of Sulṭān Bahādur Shāh's nephew, Sulṭān Maḥmūd III. Sulṭān Maḥmūd III, after inheriting the throne of his uncle, continued the legacy of his dynasty, a task possible through the loyalty of Dilāwar Khān.

Recognising Dilāwar Khān's exceptional capabilities, Sulṭān Maḥmūd III appointed him as the captain and commander of his personal bodyguard elite. This elite force, forming 12,000 soldiers, was entrusted with the critical responsibility of safeguarding the Sulṭān. As their leader, Dilāwar Khān exemplified valour and dedication to his duty, honouring his oath till death on the battlefield, his final act underlining the courageous spirit that marked his life of service.

Yāqūt Sibit Khān Ḥabashī

Yāqūt Sibit Khān Ḥabashī, also known as Ulugh Khān II or Yaqūt Begī Sulṭānī, is another notable figure of the African diaspora who shared the Ulugh Khān title. Hailing from East Africa, Yāqūt proved himself an indispensable asset to the ruling dynasty. Upon his arrival, Yāqūt swiftly ascended to a position of power, serving as vizier for Sulṭān Maḥmūd Shāh. Following the death of Mandal Dilāwar Khān, Yāqūt adopted the title of 'Ulugh Khān II', taking on the mantle of leadership and continuing the legacy of African involvement in the Sultanate's administration. He assumed command of an exclusive Ḥabashī force, previously under the leadership of Imdād al-Mulk Arslān. This force, composed entirely of Africans, is a testament to the pivotal role Africans played in the subcontinent's militaries. Yāqūt's life came to an end in 1558 AD. His final resting place is next to Bilāl Jhujhar Khān, a fitting tribute to their shared African heritage and contributions to their adopted homeland.

Shams ad-Dawlah Muḥammad al-Ḥabashī

Shams al-Dawlah Muḥammad al-Ḥabashī, known as Ulugh Khān III or Khayrāt Khān, held the title of his two predecessors among other grand honorifics. 'Shams ad-Dawlah', for instance, translates to 'Sun of the State', while his other title, 'Majlis al-Ashraf al-'Ālī', means 'Council of the High Nobility' both emphasising his significant role in the governance of the state. He was the son of Yāqūt Sibit Ulugh Khān II and followed in his father's footsteps, serving as vizier from 1543 AD to 1557-8 AD. As a patron of the arts and scholarship, he supported the renowned author Al-Ḥājī ad-Dabīr, the author of 'Tārīkh Gujurāt'. His patronage not only promoted intellectual pursuits but also added to the cultural richness of the period.

Continuing the tradition of entrusting high-ranking positions to fellow Africans, Muḥammad Ulugh Khān III appointed Bilāl Falāḥ Khān Ḥabashī as his vizier. This appointment fostered loyalty among the Ḥabashī troops and officers, further joining the African influence within the Sultanate.

Shaykh Sa'īd al-Ḥabashī Sulṭānī

Shaykh Sa'īd al-Ḥabashī Sulṭānī, who passed away in 1576 AD, was a remarkable figure. He began his career in the retinue of General Aḥmad Shāh Bilāl Jhujhar Khān in approximately 1554 AD. He then served as a general in the army of the last Sultan, Shams ad-Dīn Muẓaffar Shāh III, of the Gujarāt Sultanate until its annexation by the Mughal Empire in 1573 AD. Shaykh Saʿīd, thereafter, retired to Ahmedabad, in Gujarāt, as a wealthy man after a distinguished military career.

Over the course of his career, Siddī Saʿīd ascended the social ranks to become a prominent nobleman. He amassed a library, owned over a hundred slaves, made the Ḥajj pilgrimage, and built a mosque in 1573 AD and started a langar (public kitchen) for the poor in its vicinity, an act of philanthropy in line with his devout faith.

His final resting place was chosen to be near this mosque, and he was buried there following his death three years after its construction in 1576 AD. The construction of the mosque occurred in the final year of the Gujarāt Sultanate's existence. However, during the Mārāthā rule, the mosque fell into disrepair. Under British Colonial rule, it served as an office for the Mamlatdar of Daskroi-taluka. Later, during a visit to Ahmedabad, Lord Curzon, the then Viceroy of India, ordered the vacation of the premises as part of his preservation policies.

The Siddī Sayyid Mosque is famed for its ten intricately carved stone lattice work windows, locally known as 'jālīs', on the side and rear arches. The rear wall is filled with square stone pierced panels in geometric designs. The two bays flanking the central aisle have reticulated stone slabs carved in designs of intertwined trees and foliage and a palm motif. This mosque has become an unofficial symbol of the city of Ahmedabad, and its lattice design inspired the logo of the Indian Institute of Management, Ahmedabad.

Bābā Ghor

Bābā Ghor, known as 'Bāvā Gor' in Western India, is a revered figure who is believed to have come to Gujarāt from East Africa around the 13th century AD. In addition to his status as a saint and spiritual ancestor of the Siddī community, he is also credited with developing the Agate bead industry in the region. Agate, a hard, fine-grained variegated chalcedony stone, is characterised by its distinctive stripes of colour. It has been used extensively in jewellery and ornamentation. Bāvā Gor is said to have pioneered the craft of bead making with this stone, imparting his knowledge to others and thereby laying the foundation for an industry that would flourish for centuries.

There are varied narratives about Bāvā Gor's life and exploits. According to one account, he was an illuminated saint who came up with the idea of bead-making during meditation. Another account portrays him as a military leader who journeyed from Makkah to India with his Ḥabashī relatives on a holy religious mission. Regardless of the differing tales, Bāvā Gor's impact in Gujarāt is clear even today. His grave has become a powerful symbol, standing for the only Muslim power or centre in an area primarily under Hindu rule.

In 1819, Lieutenant Copland, a British officer, described it as a place of reverence for local miners and bead makers. Every year, bead workers honour Bāvā Gor's legacy by taking a day off to feed the poor Siddīs in the area, known as the "children of Bāvā". His grave is visited by Muslims, Hindus and Christians, from all over India, who come to celebrate his life and accomplishments. They engage in dances and play goma music and, knowingly or unknowingly, celebrate Bāvā Gor's African roots.

Mālik 'Ambar

Mālik 'Ambar, originally named Chāpū, was born in Harar, 'Adāl Sultanate, in 1548 AD. He belonged to the Mayan ethnic group, who were well known in their homeland as skilled warriors and often served as mercenaries in regional wars. As a child, he was enslaved in Zaylaʿ, Somalia, taken to Yemen and then later sold in Baghdad to the Qāḍī al-Quḍāt (Chief Judge) of Makkah. Thereafter, he was sold to Mīr Qāsim al-Baghdādī. Noticing 'Ambar's superior intellectual qualities, Mīr Qāsim converted him to Islām and renamed him "Ambar' before taking him to India. 'Ambar was well educated, refined, and highly skilled, with abilities in over five languages at a very young age. Once in India, he showed his exceptional strategic and leadership abilities as he served as the regent of the Niẓāmshāhī dynasty of Ahmednagar from 1607 AD to 1626 AD. This dynasty was a significant power in the Deccan region during the late 15th to early 17th century AD, known for its resistance to the expansion of the Mughal Empire. He played a crucial role in enhancing the strength and power of Murtazā Niẓām Shāh II, raising a formidable army for the Sulṭān. Starting from a cavalry of just 150, he managed to grow it to 7,000 in a relatively short time. This expansion did not stop there; by 1610 AD, his army had grown to include 10,000 Ḥabashīs and 40,000 Deccanīs. He also shifted the capital from Paranda to Junnar and set up a new city, Khadkī, which was later renamed 'Aurangabād' by Emperor Aurangzēb during his invasion of the Deccan from 1658 AD to 1707 AD.

Mālik 'Ambar also had the foresight to appoint puppet sultans to repel the ongoing Mughal attacks from the North, a move that revitalised the Ahmednagar sultanate. He proved to be a formidable adversary to the Mughal emperor, Jahāngīr, successfully thwarting Jahāngīr's many attempts to conquer the kingdom. His bold defensive strategy, illustrated by his use of a complex network of fortifications and mobile artillery, coupled with the use of guerrilla warfare tactics, known as 'bargī gīrī', kept the mighty Mughals at bay.

Mālik 'Ambar passed away in 1626 AD at the age of 77. His tomb is located in Khuldabād, near the shrine of the famous Ṣūfī saint, Zār Zārī Baksh. Interestingly, many paintings of Mālik 'Ambar have survived, such as the one used for the cover of this book, faithfully depicting his African features.

He and his Siddī wife, Bībī Karīmah, had two sons, Fāteḥ Khān and Changīz Khān, and two daughters. His eldest and youngest daughters were named Shahīr Bano and Azīja Bano, respectively. Azīja Bano was married to a nobleman named Siddī 'Abdullāh. One of them was married to a prince of the Ahmednagar royal family who, with 'Ambar's aid, was later crowned as Sulṭān Murtazā Niẓām Shāh II. His youngest daughter was married to the Circassian Commander of the Ahmednagar army, Muqarrab Khān, who later became a general under the Mughal Emperor and received the title 'Rustam Khān Bahādur Fīrawz Jang'. Fāteḥ Khān succeeded his father as the regent of the Niẓām Shāhs. However, the sons' lack of their father's military and political capabilities, coupled with a series of internal struggles among the nobility, led to the sultanate's fall to the Mughal Empire within ten years of 'Ambar's death.

Ikhlāṣ Khān

Ikhlāṣ Khān was another prominent African figure in the Deccan region during the late 16th and early 17th centuries AD, serving as the Prime Minister of Bijapūr during the reign of Sulṭān Ibrāhīm ʿĀdil Shāh II and later Muḥammad ʿĀdil Shāh.

Initially, Ikhlāṣ Khān served as a functionary under Sulṭān Ibrāhīm ʿĀdil Shāh II, giving petitions and even carrying out assassinations at the ruler's behest. His capabilities led to his appointment as the finance minister and commander of the army, roles that saw him expand Bijapūr's territory into Mysore. Later, Khān was made the regent to the Sulṭān's son, Aḥmad Shāh, ruling on Aḥmad's behalf until he was ready to assume the throne.

In 1595 AD, Ikhlāṣ Khān tried a coup to place Aḥmad Shāh on the throne and later tried, unsuccessfully, to depose Aḥmad and replace him with his own puppet, Mūtī Shāh. Despite this failure, Khān managed to hold onto his power and went ahead to cut his rivals within Bijapūr, ultimately establishing himself as the kingdom's absolute ruler. However, his reign was not without challenges. His grip on power eventually disintegrated, leading to his defeat in the Battle of Bhātwadī in 1624 AD. Despite this, he was still honoured with the title 'Ikhlāṣ Khān' in 1635 AD and appointed as the governor of a province bordering Golconda. The final details of his life remain unclear, but it is generally agreed that he died approximately 1656 AD, perhaps serving at that last posting.

The Ḥabashī Dynasty of Bengal

The Ḥabashī Dynasty refers to a brief period in the history of Bengal, currently spanning regions of Bangladesh and the Indian state of West Bengal when Ethiopian Abyssinian rulers held power. Their reign stretched from 1487 AD to 1493 or 1494 AD in the Bengal Sultanate following an uprising against and the next assassination of Jalāluddīn Fāteḥ Shāh from the Ilyās Shāhī Dynasty.

The Ilyās Shāhī Dynasty was founded by Shams ad-Dīn Ilyās Shāh and reigned over the autonomous medieval Islāmic Bengal Sultanate from 1352 AD to 1487 AD. As its founder, Ilyās Shāh was an assertive ruler who focused on strengthening his rule over Bengal and its surrounding areas. He launched several military campaigns, integrating both sovereign and smaller tributary states to broaden his dominion. These territories included regions of Bihār, Jhārkhānd, and Orīssā, which are part of modern-day India.

During this era, many Abyssinian (Ḥabashī) slaves were enlisted in the Bengal Sulṭān's army. Some of them ascended to high-ranking administrative roles, such as court magistrates and tax collectors. Under Jalāluddīn Fāteḥ Shāh's reign, these slaves were made palace guards, gradually gaining influence. Despite Jalāluddīn's attempts to control them, the Ḥabashīs revolted, assassinated the Sulṭān and took over the throne.

Among these Ḥabashīs was a eunuch slave, Bārbak, who rose through the ranks to become the commander of the palace guards. He orchestrated the rebellion against Sulṭān Fāteḥ Shāh. Bārbak assumed power in 1487 AD, effectively founding the Ḥabashī dynasty in Bengal. He adopted the title Sulṭān Shāhzādāh and the title 'Ghiyāsuddīn Bārbak Shāh'. His time as a ruler was cut short when he was murdered in the same year by Saifuddīn Fīrawz Shāh, also an Abyssinian eunuch, who was a supporter of the Ilyās Shāhī dynasty and served as the commander of the army. Despite the brevity of his reign, some coins have been discovered that bear his name.

Following Bārbak's assassination, Mālik Andil Ḥabashī, who served as an army commander during the Ilyās Shāhī dynasty, better known as Saifuddīn Fīrawz Shāh, ascended the throne. Once in power, he assumed the title 'Saifuddīn Fīrawz Shāh' and, given his predecessor's short reign, is regarded as the true founder of Ḥabashī rule in Bengal.

Saifuddīn Fīrawz Shāh made significant contributions to architecture and calligraphy in Bengal. He commissioned the construction of several mosques, including one in Māldā built by Majlis Saʿd and a ten-domed mosque in Goa Matli, Māldā. He is also associated with the construction of forts in Bokainagar and Tājpūr, which were set up during an expedition to Kāmārūpā by Majlis Khān Humāyūn under Fīrawz Shāh's orders. One of Fīrawz Shāh's most notable architectural achievements is the Fīrawz Mīnār, a five-story tower found in Gaūdā. Construction began in 1485 AD, before his reign, and was completed in 1489 AD to commemorate his battlefield victories. According to a popular tradition, despite its magnificence, Fīrawz Shāh threw the chief architect from the top story of the tower, displeased with its height.

Fīrawz Shāh ruled for two years until his death in 1489 AD. He was succeeded by his adopted son, Maḥmūd Shāh II. While most historians believe he died of natural causes, some sources, such as Ghulām Ḥusain Salīm and Jadūnāth Sarkār, suggest that he might have been assassinated by one of the Abyssinian palace guards.

Maḥmūd Shāh II, an infant, assumed the role of Sulṭān of Bengal in 1489 AD. With him being too young to rule, Ḥabsh Khān, an influential court figure, became his regent. However, their reign was abruptly ended in 1490 AD by Siddī Badr, another Ḥabashī who held power as the Sulṭān of Bengal until 1494 AD. Once upon the throne, he adopted the title of 'Shams ud-Dīn Muẓaffar Shāh'. He was described by Indo-Persian historians as a tyrant whose cruelty led to him becoming deeply unpopular among both the nobles and commoners of Bengal. During his reign, Muẓaffar Shāh amassed a formidable army of 30,000 soldiers, which included thousands of Afghans and 5,000 Abyssinians. In 1490-1491 AD, he constructed a mosque in Gangarīmpūr near the Dargah of Makhdūm Mawlānā 'Aṭā. His governor, Khurshīd Khān, established a Jāmiʿ

Mosque near Nawābganj on the banks of the Māhānāndā River in December 1492 AD. In 1492-93 AD, Muẓaffar Shāh defeated the Kāmatā Kingdom and annexed their territories, later issuing coins that bore the inscription "Kāmatā Mardān 898". On 2nd July 1493 AD, the Sulṭān constructed a building close to the dargah of Nūr Quṭb 'Ālam in Hazrat Pānduā.

His reign came to a sudden end in 1494 AD when his vizier, Sayyid Ḥusain, led, as was the fate of his many predecessors, a rebellion against him. Muẓaffar Shāh was killed in the rebellion, and Ḥusain succeeded him as Sulṭān, adopting the name "Alā'uddīn Ḥusain Shāh'. He set up the Ḥusain Shāhī dynasty of Bengal and removed all Ḥabashīs from administrative posts, marking the end of Ḥabashī rule in Bengal. This led many of these Ḥabashīs to later migrate to Gujarāt and Deccan.

The Ḥabashī Dynasty's existence highlights the presence and influence of Africans outside of the African continent, specifically in Asia. It is a testament to the long history of the African diaspora and its significance in shaping world history. Despite the challenges they faced in terms of racial prejudice, the Ḥabashīs were able to ascend to the highest echelons of power in a society different from their own.

The knowledge that Bengal once had African kings challenges prevailing notions of history and power, offering an essential perspective in understanding the complexities of racial dynamics. Although no longer kings, the Siddī people in the subcontinent have managed to preserve their African lineage, heritage, language, culture, and dances despite the challenges they have faced. They have kept their African languages alive and have managed to support their traditional dances, characterised by vibrant rhythms, energetic movements, and storytelling elements, all to express their history, emotions, and collective experiences. Some Siddīs have even formed dance troops and cultural groups that tour Europe, highlighting their rich traditions and captivating audiences with their performances. The Siddīs' commitment to preserving their African lineage and cultural practices serves as a source of pride and empowerment for their community. It is a powerful resistance against the erasure of black history and an affirmation of their unique identity within the diverse fabric of the subcontinent.

As we draw the curtains on our exploration of the intricate and profound relationship between Islāmic Africa, Asia, and the Middle East, it becomes evident that the threads of Black history are woven deeply into the tapestry of the Muslim World. From the dunes of Arabia to the palaces of India, the imprints of Black Muslims are not just a page or a chapter but entire volumes of history that often remain overlooked.

In pre-Islāmic Arabia, Black heroes shaped the destinies of tribes and kingdoms. Their stories, whether as poets who captured the spirit of the age or as warriors whose valour became legendary, provide a vibrant testament to the diversity and dynamism of the Arabian Peninsula. The confluence of African and Arab cultures, especially in those early days, showcased a unity in diversity that transcended contemporary understandings of race and identity.

Moving forward into the Islāmic empires of the Middle Ages, Black intellectuals and revolutionaries emerged as influential figures. Their sagas, sometimes marred by challenges, other times illuminated by achievements, are a testament to their indomitable spirit. The Muftīs, scholars, and narrators who rose to prominence from African roots became essential contributors to the vast corpus of Islāmic thought and jurisprudence. Their teachings continue to echo in Islāmic seminaries and in the hearts of the faithful.

The story of Islām in East Africa is another radiant thread in this tale. From Allāh Almighty incorporating words from East African languages into the Qur'ān and the Prophet ﷺ himself entrusting the Christian King Najāshī of the Kingdom of Axum with the safety of his early followers and relatives when persecution intensified in Makkah, to Najāshī then not only offering refuge but also sending gifts and the Banū Arfidah delegation to Madīnah, this relationship enriched the city and mosque of the Prophet ﷺ, with traditional African songs and dances, weaving African traditions seamlessly into the tapestry of early Islāmic culture and exemplifying Islām's universality and embrace of diverse traditions. Thereafter, as Islām spread across the Horn of Africa and down to the Swāḥilī Coast, it melded with indigenous cultures, birthing a unique blend of traditions, languages, and architecture. The mosques of Kilwah, the poetry of Lamu, and the trade routes of Mogadishu stand as historical markers of this synthesis.

But perhaps one of the most intriguing aspects of this journey has been the realisation of East Africa's impact on the distant lands of India, Pakistan, and Bangladesh. From East African kings who ruled vast territories to saints who spread the spiritual essence of Islām, their legacies are still palpable. Cities enriched by African culture, festivals bearing African imprints, and communities cherishing their East African origins serve as living chronicles of this past.

In concluding this volume, it is essential to recognise that our endeavour is not merely a historical reconstruction, rather, it is a call to acknowledge the richness of Black legacy within the Muslim world, to dispel ignorance, and to forge a future built on mutual respect and understanding. The stories recounted here are a testament to the timeless principle that diversity is a strength, and unity can be achieved without uniformity.

As you turn the last page of this book, it is my hope that you carry forward not just knowledge but a sense of responsibility. Let us celebrate the heroes, revive the forgotten tales, and ensure that future generations recognise the intertwined destinies of Africa and Asia in the annals of Islām.

May the lessons from the past illuminate our path forward, and may the stories of unity, resilience, and brilliance inspire generations to come to actualise the profound wisdom of the Qur'ānic verse, "*Oh Mankind! Indeed, We created you from a male and a female, and made you into peoples and tribes so that you may know one another.*" [Qur'ān 49:13].

SELECTED BIBLIOGRAPHY

Jāḥiẓ, Al-. Fakhr as-Sūdān ʿalā al-Biḍān (The Glory of the Black Race over the White Race). Dar Al-Fikr, 2009.

Al-Khayyun, Rashid. Athar al-Sud fi al-Hadarah al-Islamiyyah (The Impact of the Blacks on Islamic Civilisation). Dar al-Ma'arifa, 1998.

Ali, Omar H. The African Diaspora in the Indian Ocean World. Oxford University Press, 2015.

Badawi, Abduh. Ash-Shuʿarāʾ as-Sūd wa Khasāʾiṣuhum fī ish-Shiʿri il-ʿArabī (The Black Poets and Their Characteristics in Arabic Poetry). Al-Maktaba Al-Asriyya, 2006.

Chaudhuri, K.N. Trade and Civilisation in the Indian Ocean: An Economic History from the Rise of Islam to 1750. Cambridge University Press, 1985.

El Hamel, Chouki. Black Morocco: A History of Slavery, Race, and Islam. Cambridge University Press, 2012.

Freeman-Grenville, G.S.P. East African Coast: Select Documents from the First to the Earlier Nineteenth Century. Markus Wiener Publishers, 2002.

Gurner, J.D. Sheedis: The African Diaspora in India. Asian Studies Press, 2010.

Haseeb, Khair El-Din. The Arabs and Africa. Croom Helm, 1985.

Horton, Mark. The Swahili: The Social Landscape of a Mercantile Society. Blackwell, 2001.

Hunwick, John. Islam's Black Slaves: The Other Black Diaspora. Markus Wiener Publishers, 2004.

Ibn Al-Jawzi, Abu Al-Faraj. Tanwīr al-Ghabsh fī Faḍli is-Sūdān wa al-Ḥabash (Illuminating the Darkness Regarding the Merits of the Blacks and Abyssinians). Maktaba Al-Thaqafa Al-Diniyya, 2001.

Lapidus, Ira M. Islamic Societies to the Nineteenth Century: A Global History. Cambridge University Press, 2012.

Levtzion, Nehemia. The History of Islam in Africa. Ohio University Press, 2000.

MacGaffey, Wyatt. Muslims and Chiefs in West Africa. Clarendon Press, 1987.

Manning, Patrick. The African Diaspora: A History Through Culture. Columbia University Press, 2009.

Mazrui, Ahmed A. and Christophe Wondji. The History of Islam in East Africa. UNESCO Press, 1993.

Pankhurst, Richard. The Ethiopian Borderlands: Essays in Regional History. The Red Sea Press, 1997.

Rashidi, Runoko. The African Presence in Early Asia. Transaction Publishers, 1995.

Robinson, David. Muslim Societies in African History. Cambridge University Press, 2004.

Silverstein, Adam J. Islamic History: A Very Short Introduction. Oxford University Press, 2010.

Suyuti, Jalaluddin Abdul Rahman Al-. Raf'u Shȧni il-Ḥabshān (Elevating the Status of the Abyssinians). Dar Al-Turath, 1980.

Van Sertima, Ivan. Golden Age of the Moor. Transaction Publishers, 1992.

Varela, Elsa. The African Kings: Treasures of the World. Thames & Hudson, 1997.

Made in United States
Cleveland, OH
27 October 2024

10326008R20101